ENCRYPTING
BILLIONS

ENCRYPTING BILLIONS

*How Michael Keresman
Made Cleveland the
Epicenter of E-Commerce*

Patrick R. Alexander

Legenderry Communications
Cleveland

For permission requests and special discounts on quantity purchases by corporations, associations, and others, contact:
Pralexander79@yahoo.com

ISBN 978-0-578-86661-1

Printed in the United States of America
1.5

Contents

Michael Keresman credits John Carroll University for cultivating the skills he needed for an authentic and unparalleled career in entrepreneurship. This respected Jesuit college where Keresman serves as a trustee sits majestically in the Cleveland suburb known appropriately as University Heights. But as Keresman recently perceived, "I doubt I would even be admitted to my beloved alma mater John Carroll University today." In recent years, high school students with C and B level scores are discouraged from even applying to influential or well-known colleges. Many higher learning institutions are forced to juggle the fundamentals of education with an appearance of being more "elite." Perhaps Keresman would fix this conundrum facing the educational world. Keresman believes, "It would be a shame if high level thinkers plagued with average grades are continuously relegated away from schools like John Carroll." Keresman laments, "Brains are similar to bodies; they don't always mature in high school."

Photo Patrick R. Alexander, 2018

Not Like Us

I first learned about Michael Keresman while playing golf at a club in Cleveland. Described as the "internet security guy," Michael had been fairly conspicuous roaming the grounds. Indulgence may be an understatement. Michael really enjoys playing golf. Plus, stories about his Rolodex were legendary (if you don't know what a Rolodex is, look it up). Either way, Michael Keresman likes to golf, drink, smoke and converse; in any order you prefer, Michael does all of these very well. His entertaining at the club has been boundless. Heck, one-time, Keresman hosted F. Lee Bailey at the club. Yes, that F. Lee Bailey, O.J. Simpson's attorney. Even Alice Cooper played a round of golf with him. Actually, these three men, The Attorney, The Rocker, The Entrepreneur are more similar than you may think. But that's not this book.

Michael A. Keresman, who founded and led CardinalCommerce for roughly 18 years, is an emblematic figure of the kind of entrepreneurs found in Silicon Valley. Only Keresman wasn't in Silicon Valley; he was in Cleveland, Ohio. At the time the big rumor in Cleveland was that Visa was buying Keresman's company. Many business insiders and leaders all around the north coast were curious. Why would a massive company like Visa buy a seemingly minor company so far away from the epicenter of internet intellectual property ownership? Cardinal had about 170 employees at the time. Crain's Cleveland Business, the local business magazine and The Cleveland Plain Dealer, the daily newspaper, struggled to answer this question. The year was 2017.

What was it about CardinalCommerce or Keresman that interested a world class brand like Visa? Interestingly, the news outlets did secure one noteworthy fact—Visa's future plans for Cardinal and all of its dedicated employees. According to the newspapers, Visa was going to insist

CardinalCommerce stay in Mentor, Ohio. Mentor is a thriving eastern suburb of Cleveland along the shore of Lake Erie. It's just minutes to downtown Cleveland by freeway. However, as this story develops, you will see northeast Ohio becomes a key factor for this amazing innovative company and Keresman's subsequent breathtaking transaction. The "what's so special about Cleveland" perspective seemed to elude the local journalists at the time. However, Keresman always knew Cleveland would be essential to the success of his business. In fact, Keresman planned it this way from the very beginning way back in 1999.

We may recall back in 1999, Steve Jobs was making a massive comeback with Apple Computer. In just a few years, Mr. Jobs would secure a new world order; one we now hold in the palm of our hands. How ironic, this slogan from Visa, "Everywhere You Want to Be" feels today. However, Keresman at the time was focused or I should say fixated on solving a different issue with the internet.

Remember the 1990s version of the internet, the "You've Got Mail" internet? Keresman realized it could be more, much more. Keresman risked everything and built a technology company called CardinalCommerce. Now here is the amazing part: His company transformed just about everything in e-commerce. His company conceived and designed well over 100 patents that validated the authenticity of the customer to the merchant and bank. More than likely, you never heard of CardinalCommerce. But you've heard of Visa. Actually, when Visa and Mastercard first learned about CardinalCommerce and Michael Keresman, they scoffed at his little ideas and ambitions for "how things are supposed to be." This brush off from the corporate giants may have been similar to the story of a Philistine warrior and a certain shepherd boy. I'm sure you remember the story of David and Goliath!

By the time of the sale to Visa in 2017, Keresman had become somewhat of a local celebrity in the local business community. Frankly, this was not the first time his name appeared glowingly in the Cleveland business papers. Just prior to founding of CardinalCommerce, Keresman was a co-founder of the STERIS Corporation. Maybe you have heard of STERIS; a multibillion-dollar healthcare related company and a splendid specimen of contemporary entrepreneurship. Just prior to that and similar to STERIS in a way, Keresman was hidden inside another innovation of entrepreneurship related to the health care industry. Keresman was intimately involved in the success of the first statewide Health Maintenance Organization or HMO, called Group Health Plan of Northeast Ohio. This enterprise became a part of a much bigger organization known to the world as HealthAmerica. Actually, it was here at the HMO where Keresman learned the importance of using the media to one's advantage.

Some might think Keresman was trained in advertising or marketing. However, his college degree is not in public relations, communications or anything like that. His degree from John Carroll University was in finance. However, Keresman's use of the press, or as one colleague put it, "Michael's flagrant manipulation of momentum for personal and business growth through the press should be a doctorate level degree found in a media savvy school like USC."

In short, Keresman had to be on his game with the media. That's how Keresman created "street-cred" as he exploited a time-honored tradition known to most entrepreneurs as private placement funding. Some call it OPM—other people's money. There were multiple years involved; from 2000 to 2007 and then again from 2010 to 2013. Keresman ran up a rather hefty price tag for CardinalCommerce. Estimates were made at over $30 million. For Cleveland, in the private funding world, that's a lot of money. However, make no mistake, Keresman personally contributed to Cardinal's treasuries repeatedly throughout these rounds as well. Keresman's personal support, image and reputation were inexorably aligned alongside Cardinal's. To his adoring fans among shareholders, employees and steadfast board members, an ample reward would follow.

When people say, "a dream come true," they may be trying to explain what they believe is the life of Michael Keresman today. However, the real dream come true, CardinalCommerce, had to first wreak havoc on the titans of the financial industry. This comes with lifelong consequences. These are sacrifices, to be certain. Because of this, the Keresman story can be shocking. To win at this game one must first understand commitment. One must study and know thyself. Frankly, one must be relentless! Perhaps this may help you understand what we are dealing with here. Michael recalls a lesson he learned in high school competition.

The skill or luck of your opponent can never offend. Attitude is important in winning and being offended makes you a victim. Victims seldom win.
—Michael Keresman, 2018

The keepers of the status quo in the monetary world were overtly "offended" by Keresman. Then, CardinalCommerce advanced proprietary technology that could not be overlooked. This is not a clandestine world. This was, and is, a domain of in-your-face business giants and egos. Corporate jets, country clubs, and bottles of gin costing $700 were commonplace. Although, I have ascertained, the shenanigans familiar to us in movies like "The Wolf of Wall Street," or "Margin Call" were only vaguely played out in a similar fashion. And, I should be clear, while these things are entertaining to watch on the movie screen, you are not going to read any of that here. The scintillating private lives are just that, private.

As we go forward with the Keresman story, we should reflect on the new millennia era. After the Y2K folly, the world longed for a fresh start. Borrowing a football metaphor, the year 2000 was mostly a "head fake." What ensued thereafter was nothing less than trauma, drama and turmoil. In those 18 years while Keresman was building CardinalCommerce we witnessed the dot com bubble, the heinous terrorism strike of 9/11, two stock market crashes, humongous bank bailouts, the iPhone revolution, a 30% real estate collapse and, of course, energy and health care manipulations beyond most Americans' wildest imaginations. Even now as we pick up the pieces after the COVID pandemic, the good and the bad are debated again and again.

CardinalCommerce is a story with delicate breaks and nuances. Mistakes made were quickly erased with relentless pursuits of exceptionalism. Frankly, this is exactly what many of us need to better our careers and our businesses. C-level executives and all entrepreneurs, both young and old, will find a plethora of ideas to enhance their management for excellence. You are about to learn the many tactical techniques cultivated by Michael A. Keresman over a lifetime of legendary entrepreneurship.

However, please note, Keresman was then, and still is now, an enigma. The man is both exceptionally social and fiercely private. The variance in descriptions made from business associates, employees, fellow entrepreneurs, board members, family, friends and shareholders can range dramatically. Even today people ask, "What's Michael really like?" Well, I can say with some authority and as the reason I wrote this book, Michael A. Keresman is nothing like us.

How is This World
Supposed to Be?

Lake Erie College stands on a knoll above the great lake that shares its name. This celebrated liberal arts institution invited Michael A. Keresman to be the keynote speaker at its commencement in the late spring of 2018. Today the coeducational school has 63 programs of study for undergraduate students. Also, the school offers master's programs in education and physician assistant studies, as well as the IACBE-accredited Parker Master of Business Administration program. From this perspective Lake Erie College looks fairly normal. However, the truth—Lake Erie College is anything but normal.

Founded in 1856, this school completely transformed the tradition and foundation of the education industry. The school was not coeducational at its founding. Lake Erie College was for women only. For that era and at the school's core was a profound notion; that women could do more than first imagined to help advance humanity. The school postulated that society has modern and innovative objectives for women. The founders asked, "Are women not capable of significant intellectual improvement too?" Whether in business and finance, engineering and medicine, education and the arts, they believed women were destined for substantial contributions to our vibrant and emerging world. Back in 1856 the school was named the Lake Erie Female Seminary. It was the only single-sex institution of higher education for women through-out all of the Western Reserve. One would have to travel to Massachusetts, to Mount Holyoke, to find a similar place of learning for women. After all, this was its sister seminary from that era.

You see, Michael Keresman also knows a thing or two about challenging the establishment. Michael knows the ramifications of challenging the status quo. And just like the trailblazing women of 1856, Michael knows what it means to be untested, to be looked down upon, to be subjugated by a system that suppresses new concepts or ideas. Michael knows the fundamentals that give the status quo lasting power and influence. Michael studies incessantly how the status quo ensnares. Ironically, few appreciate that Michael felt outmatched throughout his life. However, for Michael, being a victim was not an option. More importantly, he fully understood all the ramifications of the conflicts that would arise should he wish to compete at a high level. And there is no way anyone can stop Michael Keresman from competing. Still to this day, Michael must challenge; he must draw that line in the sand. All entrepreneurs seem to share this quality; it is who they really are at their core. Nevertheless, Lake Erie College and its commencement speaker for 2018—it's a near perfect match.

Actually, there may be a pattern here with regards to the guest orators at this particular school. One that began as far back as 1861. History chronicles another prominent person for a public address at the school. This person had similar feelings about the status quo. He asked, "How is this world supposed to be?" The only difference being his national influence had yet to be etched. His name was Abraham Lincoln. It has been suggested that the newly elected president of the United States was so enamored with the progressive nature of this pioneering institution, that he felt it should be so honored and praised with a visit.

Given all we see here, perhaps more investigation should follow. Let's delve a little further at the campus of Lake Erie College. And just maybe we can get a glimpse of what Michael Keresman might want to say in "his" historic address.

The school is just a stone's throw from the center of Painesville, Ohio—situated about 30 minutes from downtown Cleveland. The property is beautifully adorned with both sturdy deciduous and delicate flowering trees. Classroom buildings and dormitories are sprinkled randomly throughout, as a few architectural worlds collide here. Stone and brick and new postmodern glass and steel structures intermingle with other ostentatious classic architecture throughout the 52-acre parcel of land.

The first building constructed on the campus in the early 1850s is a magnificent brick edifice, an Italianate building, assigned on the National Register of Historic Places. The grand four-story red brick structure is massive, serving as the iconic pictogram on all of the college's publications today. Here, the many aspects of history radiate. This College Hall famously became a grand stop for many old-world presidents, governors, dignitaries, and all the world's great industrialists from the 1800s. People ask, did Lincoln, Garfield, or McKinley actually set foot here? Yes, for two out of three. History states that Lincoln never left the train station; the adoring fans were so substantial it was impractical to even try. With regards to Lincoln, what should have taken place at College Hall at the Lake Erie Female Seminary had to wait for another time. His world was in turmoil. It was February 1861, and Lincoln needed to be back in Washington, D.C.

Today, College Hall of Lake Erie College feels more dignified than opulent. Although it would be easy to imagine a high society gathering from the late 1800s taking place here; few realize, the emerging city of Cleveland and all of northeast Ohio became a powerhouse of commercial energy back then. In the 1870s and 1880s, half of the millionaires in the world lived in downtown Cleveland. Rockefeller, Payne, and Carnegie, all had homes on Euclid Avenue, better known as "Millionaires' Row." This beautiful, old-world thoroughfare, adorned with luxurious Tudor and stone estates, is all but forgotten. Many believe this era established all the world-class businesses and industries that became the firmament for today's modern companies. These business leaders left their fingerprints all over our modern world.

These men, for the most part, were often described as refined, cultured, and gentlemanly. It was their entrepreneurial geniuses that molded a new society. They did so by constructing world class companies and countless numbers of libraries, hospitals, museums, and higher learning institutions just like The Lake Erie Female Seminary of 1856. They too daringly asked, "How is our world supposed to be?"

Today, it's somewhat comforting that Lake Erie College sustains the many facets of its noteworthy historical significance. This can be found with another architectural peculiarity on the campus known as Memorial Hall. The Bedford limestone construction and the 25-foot pillars that stand on either side of the entrance are reminiscent of the freemasonry architectural style. The colorful past, once again, is evident immediately because here we see a common Greek design. Names of famous composers have been carved randomly on the massive sandstone blocks of its exterior walls. The many famous musicians who have played on its stage are the very fabric of music history itself. In addition, a plaque on the wall declares that this wonderful building served all the people of Ohio when the Ohio Supreme Court held its assemblies here in April of 1978.

The stateliness of Memorial Hall with its 800-person seating capacity serves Lake Erie College during convocations, artistic performances, lecture series and other special occasions. Considered acoustically as one of the best small concert halls in the world, it houses a magnificent six-division E.M. Skinner organ built in 1927. Perhaps you can imagine sitting in this old college gallery, fortified by stone blocks and columns erected a century ago. This lecture hall feels more like a church with narrow two-story windows wrapped in thick, ornate, multicolored wood molding. Long pews, anchored on a raked floor situated in a slight parabola with vaulted ceilings above, make our spiritual illusion complete. The high gloss polished Philippine mahogany wood is resilient and timeless. Any movement instantly registers petite, high pitch squeaks, creaks and groans from the century old timber. The sight lines and acoustics in this lecture hall are enviable for any golden age construction. Memorial Hall would be a wonderful place to witness Michael Keresman's commencement address. Perhaps Michael will construct his commencement message based solely on his remarkable business dealings over the last 30 years.

After all, the Keresman entrepreneurial story begins well before his founding of CardinalCommerce, which is the principal thrust behind this book. Many years ago, in the early 1980s, Michael blazed a trail as a vital member of the management team that created the first state-wide Health Maintenance Organization (HMO). Here, his entrepreneurial spirits were ignited. Perhaps, Mr. Keresman will want to talk about that.

However, with the raised awareness of HMOs across the country, Michael was then seduced away and became a co-founder at the STERIS Corporation. Now he could really clean-up as CFO with this innovative medical device start-up. After all, in just 10 years, Michael helped STERIS become a billion-dollar company.

Actually, Michael may wish to talk about the years at STERIS, where his skills in entrepreneurship were challenged and tested continuously for something greater, and he knew it. A reoccurring dream (yes, literally a dream) nagged and prompted him to try something on his own. All he had in this dream was a name, Cardinal, and that he would build a company against all odds in his hometown of Cleveland, Ohio. So, in 1999 Michael left his well-paid senior executive job and became Founder, Chief Executive, and Chairman of CardinalCommerce. The financial establishment was continuously challenged as Michael and his remarkable team of overachievers created the largest digital authentication company in the world.

Cardinal's platform had the capability to compare known facts about any person initiating an internet transaction, often going over several hundred data points in the blink of an eye. Intelligent authentication assures all parties involved that this is not a fake or fraudulent transaction. Michael points out that the Cardinal software declares, "Yep, this person is a real customer. And yep, this is their real bank card. And yep, this person will ultimately pay their bill."

Michael had to have patience, confidence, wisdom and, most importantly, perseverance to challenge the status quo. Because back in 1999, these children who are graduating this year in 2018 couldn't even hold a Game Boy in their hands while Michael Keresman was thinking, "How can I make buying on the internet easy? How can I make it safe? How can I remove the unnecessary friction or burdensome verification steps?" Or should I say he thought, "How is this world supposed to be?"

Mr. Keresman began to realize that everybody would eventually be shopping online. Bank cards would need to be accepted and "authenticated" quickly. Otherwise, he thought, "the internet will be nothing more than a parlor trick." He will probably tell the students who are going to graduate here at Lake Erie College that years ago, business was entirely generated in a face-to-face world. Even telephone orders were only a tiny, minuscule fraction of the business being conducted. For the most part, cash was the only currency.

Michael should say CardinalCommerce was built on these pivotal convictions: Buying needed to be fast, safe and secure. Michael calls it, "The Cardinal Trust." To achieve this goal the Cardinal software and the new Cardinal architecture had to be centralized away from the merchant and banks. Michael imagined this trust must be nourished and cherished in order to grow and support the insatiable flurry of demand we have today.

To grab the attention of this millennial generation, Michael needs to bring to light the current estimates for an average day of online transactions: 140 million transactions in just 24 hours. That's nearly 5,800,000 business transactions every hour, or 97,200 a minute, or 1,620.37037 transactions every second. Maybe that will impress these new graduates. Frankly, a prerequisite to online business and the only currency needed is "intelligent authentication."

Oh wait, the best part: Michael should say Cardinal's intelligent authentication software has also contributed on a grand scale to the creation of social media. The most transparent and organic of all the marketing tools was developed because of his company. Lest we forget, online reviews of every product and/or service are loaded securely by the user every second all over the world. So, across all barriers, in our world of skeptics and know-it-alls, Facebook busy-bodies, and incessant Googling-experts, what are merchants and banks finding? They are finding the ultimate prize—brand loyalty—a commerce revolution, all thanks to Michael A. Keresman and CardinalCommerce.

Of course, this is where Michael wanted to build his company. Of course, CardinalCommerce challenged the status quo. Of course, the behemoths, the Goliaths in the credit card, banking, and global merchant world were not ready for what was coming next. Michael Keresman is from Cleveland. And, just like so many times before, a Cleveland native would wind up winning a world-class horse race.

Dr. Brian Posler, president of Lake Erie College, chaired a committee that handpicked Michael Keresman to deliver the commencement address for a specific reason. I'm sure his committee was enamored with everything we see here. I'm sure they thought Michael's career would be very inspiring to this millennial generation. However, just like the men and women that established Lake Erie College so many years ago, these individuals loved their place in the world. This was Cleveland, Ohio. The rest saw Cleveland as a newcomer with incredible power, speed, and agility. Don't worry if you are the dark horse, the inexperienced colt, or the token filly. The bell rings and the gates open; future generations will reflect forever on the heart necessary to finish a race of this magnitude, the heart found in just a few.

The entrepreneurs back then had imagination, gumption, and perseverance just like the entrepreneurs of today. These are words used for the generations of people that have grown up along the shore of Lake Erie. Perhaps there is something unique to Cleveland's location and resources. Perhaps the entrepreneurial spirit that oozes out of so many from the Cleveland area also can be found in Mr. Keresman. Anyone who dares to ask, "How is this world supposed to be?" just might end up in their own cautionary tale about entrepreneurship.

Michael's complete commencement address can be found in chapter 7.

CHAPTER 1

A Super (human) Processor

No man can create a machine superior
to that fertile mind you possess.

Michael Keresman saw his first computer in 1983. In the lore, this is presented as a moment of enmity for the then 25-year-old accountant. He was positively territorial over his dominion of numbers. Ostensibly computers were infringing on his profession. At that time, Michael's senior boss, Dr. Maxwell Davis, Chairman of Group Health Plan of Northeast Ohio, called Gary Gordon, COO, and Michael Keresman, CFO, into his office. It was the springtime in Northeast Ohio. Birds were chirping and the sun was out. Gary Gordon, a thoughtful and compassionate boss, was Michael's immediate superior at the innovative health maintenance organization (HMO). Michael had been working alongside the two men for just over a year. All the traditional numbers common to the health care industry were coalescing in Michael's brain for future control. Michael was beginning to think like a good accountant. And then this happened.

Dr. Davis had just read an article in The Wall Street Journal and wanted to impart his newfound wisdom. It concerned a new-fangled, electric slide rule and calculator all wrapped into one box that excited Dr. Davis. That's right, it's all about a "personal computer," better known as the PC. Dr. Davis keenly predicted that this device was going to change our world! Dr. Davis wanted a computer for *his* company ASAP! Michael also read the article and frankly was not interested. "What will they need me for? The PC can make countless calculations every second!" Michael felt threatened. He didn't want to know anything about the PC. However, he was intrigued with the concept of any device that could make multiple calculations in an instant. Michael imagined the potential computers might have for analyzing great sums of data for the individual. How would risk be measured? Michael's imaginings moved toward odds making. But not for gambling, no, nothing like that. The discovery process; the production and assembly of analytics itself, now that was a different matter entirely.

Please acknowledge, *all* of the accounting Michael did at the time was by hand, mostly on a "10-key" or hand-held calculator. Actually, Michael was fairly proficient doing most calculations in his head! There was no Excel spreadsheet at the touch of a button. *Everything* was completed by hand. Finance and accounting students from this time were caught squarely in the middle of a revolution guided by science over education. Anyone obtaining a formal, higher education degree from the late 1970s and early 1980s understood this predicament. Truthfully, Michael was terrified by this new invention; Michael felt defenseless. Maybe computers would turn out to be a cult.

Gary Gordon researched all the PCs on the market. This took days and days. Multiple trips to stores that carried electronics, stereos and even TVs were involved. Frankly, there were no centralized computer super stores at that time. Computers were hard to find. In the end, Mr. Gordon made the purchase of a portable computer released in April 1983 hyped as the "the Compaq luggable." It weighed in at 28 pounds for an introductory price of $3,590, *but* it had a built-in 9" green-screen monitor.

Little did anyone know then that this PC would be the first of many contenders that contributed to IBM's now notorious slide a decade later. IBM, long considered to be the bluest of blue-chip stocks, would go tumbling in March of 1991. The market share developed over decades would finally erode enough to cause panic for several institutional investors. Meek individual shareholders were rattled thereafter. Please note, the IBM stock did return to normalcy, but the damage was done. Institutional investors were focusing on experimental companies on the West Coast. On their watch lists at the time: Apple, Applied Materials, Atari, Fairchild, Hewlett-Packard, Intel, Microsoft, National Semiconductor, Varian Associates, Xerox, and hundreds of other companies. The Bay Area around San Francisco would explode into the new intellectual property center of the USA. These innovative compa-

nies like Compaq were challenging the status quo. Michael took notice of the consumer sentiment of his boss Gary Gordon. He chose Compaq precisely because it wasn't an IBM!

Well, it's done. Gary Gordon did his job. He brought this "thing" to his office which, frankly, by today's standard, was not small or compact at all; it was huge. There it sat on the table in Mr. Gordon's office. Michael passed by it daily. The psychological taunting had begun. Michael even heard the damn thing talking to him. Phrases like, "You're going to be 26 and completely obsolete!" would just pop into his head. These hauntings continued day after day. The teasing persisted, "Hey Michael, I'm way faster than you!" Please note, Michael knew he wasn't going crazy. But he did think his career was in jeopardy.

The next week, Mr. Gordon was out of town on business. His office remained dark. Michael thought, "Good, now I don't have to look at the damn thing every time I pass by." That's when the light went on in his head. In typical Michael fashion, a contemplative moment occurred.

He thought, "Why am I intimidated by something I don't know anything about?"

Michael needed to devise a strategy. Michael knew he needed some time to conduct a few experiments with the electronic gadget. However, wouldn't there be scrutiny from coworkers, just general curiosity? This may turn his investigation into a carnival. Some colleagues may go so far as to say, he's not really working, he's just playing around all day. So, he did the unexpected. He concocted a way to *steal* the computer right out of the office. The risk was high. Taking any office property home was not allowed. However, Michael thought it must be done. If there is going to be any future forged together, the two must get personal.

Please remember at the time there wasn't any online support. It would take another 15 years for Larry Page and Sergey Brin to invent and launch Google. In fact, no one even heard the phrase "search engine" before. Actually, PCs were sold with huge printed guidebooks. Literally two textbooks accompanied the damn thing. Michael thought, this is crazy!

Some historic perspective may help. In the early 1980s Microsoft had about 200 employees. Total sales for the company were under $20 million or so, which is a lot of money. But still, Microsoft was not even close to becoming a household name! In an effort to keep momentum for the industry as a whole, Bill Gates publicly praised Steve Jobs for his accomplishment of the Macintosh computer. Ironically, the mainstream press scarcely acknowledged these rivals propelling one another with warp speed over the next five years. Oh and, Mark Zuckerberg was not even born yet. And get this, Michael's boss read about this new invention in a newspaper. The Wall Street Journal, the most trusted source for pertinent business information, made a bold declaration to the world. The PC, "a machine that can make thousands of calculations in a second would soon be in your home or business." Actually, computers were slow back then. Today computers do hundreds of millions of calculations in a second. Plus, the memory installed was just over 64 KB, or kilobytes. And . . . Michael needed to "steal the thing out of the office," so as to not draw too much attention upon himself while at work! Well guess what? He succeeded. Quite simply, no one noticed. After all, it wasn't just any personal computer; it was a portable computer. Either way, on that Friday, when the office became quiet, when no one was paying attention, Michael snuck his little workplace antagonist out of the building.

At first, Michael's raincoat draped over his arm provided some camouflage for "the luggable." Hard to imagine today, but this device was about the size of the baggage we drag around airports and put in overhead bins while flying. Only, the PC had no wheels. Also, Michael decided to use the stairs for his exit. Why? No one uses stairs. Michael even placed his car near the door, for a clean getaway. Michael made sure the doors were unlocked, no fumbling with car keys. Everything was going smoothly, and then Michael heard footsteps in the hallway. He waited on the landing between floors three and two. Michael slowly proceeded. "Oh, dear God, I'm going to get fired for stealing company equipment that I don't even *want!*" Michael peeked out the door. Oh, it's only Max, one of the custodians. Michael slid out the door like James Bond himself. The car door flew open and in an instant Michael was behind the wheel. Michael was on his way home to safety. It was Friday, May 27, Memorial Day weekend, 1983.

Michael did not sleep the entire weekend. Complete exhaustion set in a few hours before he needed to be back at work Tuesday morning. Every page in the manuals had been either read two times, dog-eared, or highlighted. Michael got a couple of hours of rest, then went back to the office like normal. Only everything wasn't normal. That's when Michael asked Mr. Gordon for some "software." His boss had no idea what he was talking about. Mike explained he needed Lotus 1-2-3! A week later, when Michael finally got the accounting software, everyone's life was going to change. When I say everyone, I mean everyone.

Though, let's be clear, big corporate businesses, like banks and insurance companies, were already using computers. Huge monstrosities that cost $4 million back in the 1970s were built precisely for big business and not the individual. Computers were not affordable or practical for the individual. These computers were programmed to run in languages that seemed foreign. Most programming languages were not (and are still not today) standardized by an international (or national) governing body. Even the ones used commonly are constantly being manipulated. Notable standardized programming languages like ALGOL, C, C++, JavaScript, Smalltalk, Prolog, Common Lisp, Ada, Fortran, Cobol, SQL and XQuery will never be settled.

Either way, as smaller, more affordable computers were coming forward, most people believed a confrontation with the expanding computer world was inevitable. Computers were going personal. They were destined to be in every business in the USA in less than 15 years!

People are always curious as to how the truly innovative and successful entrepreneurs learn what they learn and instinctively know what they know. Well, in Michael's case, we must return to a time before he was even born to understand how the foundation of a certain status quo was developing in the United States. We need to analyze the systems that were being jammed into place in a post-WWII economy, specifically in American health care in the 1950s. This is the very industry where Michael would first be recognized for his true hard work and analytical acumen. The "information systems" that we often take for granted in the modern world were first built in the banking, insurance and health care industries. We need to dissect in microscopic detail a fairly complicated industry to see how its influences would reshape our world two times over.

The first HMOs, like Group Health Plan of Northeast Ohio, were developed out of the Kaiser Permanente business model. During World War II, seaworthy fighting vessels were in high demand. The USA was building most of the ships in Oakland, California. The number of workers pouring into California for work was just short of astronomical. In short order, the number of workers easily outstripped the health care delivery system's capability for servicing the booming labor market. Out of desperation, Kaiser Shipbuilding began to import doctors. Having sick or injured workers traveling to other locations around the west coast was simply foolish. Rather than export patients, Kaiser began retrofitting vacant buildings into health care centers. It is important to point out that many hospitals were operating similar to today as "not for profit" institutions as hundreds of doctors from various health care disciplines and specialties were recruited from around the country to support the workers who were building the Navy to win the war.

After the war, in the early 1950s, Kaiser Shipbuilding had evolved into Kaiser Permanente. To proliferate its model, it implemented an aggressive tactic: it opened up its health care capabilities to workers other than Kaiser Shipbuilding employees. Then Kaiser Permanente began exporting what it learned during the war years, which turned out to be a pretty efficient way to deliver health care all across America. This was a game changer in health care. Today Kaiser Permanente operates 39 hospitals and more than 700 medical offices, with over 300,000 personnel, including more than 80,000 physicians and nurses.

Again, after the war California continued to grow and grow as citizens moved from East to West. The influx of new migration rivaled any other point in history, including the Gold Rush. Rust Belt cities like Cleveland were waning. The advent of air conditioning made Southern and Western states particularly attractive to newcomers. Florida, Texas, Nevada, and California were intriguing, as they had no state tax for earned income. California had become the epicenter for nearly all defense contractors. The industry was doubling in size annually as the Cold War and aerospace industries were heating up, too!

Regardless of the criticism from cynics and many status quo politicians at that time, the new health care model from Kaiser proved to be amazingly efficient. The New York Times slanderously labeled the HMO as a "doc-in-a-box." The Times subtly drew a likeness of HMO healthcare to a circus-like fast food chain known to millions on the west coast as Jack in the Box.

However, the large office buildings that were repurposed into temporary diagnosis and outpatient treatment facilities were not formal hospitals. Simple, outpatient care was administered quickly to the willing health care recipient. So, doc-in-a-box was a rhythmic way to describe this new process. This oversimplification of the health care industry completely revolutionized how the U.S. was going to spend billions and billions of dollars over the next 50 years, and here's why. A new status quo was growing in power and influence.

For starters, these HMOs provided doctors with a regular salary. House calls were inefficient, so they ceased entirely. Doctors did not have to set up their own offices. They did not need to hire support staff. Individual practitioners could specialize in whatever care or type of care brought them the most satisfaction and reward. This was how the "specialist" was born. You had a rash? "See Dr. Tim, he has a keen understanding of skin abrasions and allergies." You had a lingering cough? "See Dr. Roger. It could be this thing called a 'virus' that Russian biologist Dmitri Ivanovsky has been talking about. Or maybe, Dr. Isabel could diagnose your maladies because she specializes in anti-fungal solutions."

As you can imagine, Kaiser Permanente basically became one of the first health care conglomerates in "delivery systems" in the primary and secondary care industry. All kinds of people were closely watching this major shift and acceptance of the new health care model. Prudential, a major life insurance company, immediately followed suit and became a competitor.

Cleveland had the opposite phenomenon; it had an abundance of doctors, while patient population was starting to decline. To put a doc-in-a-box in a city like Cleveland would be competing with an entrenched network of existing physicians. Nevertheless, a group of innovative doctors banded together completely on their own. They built their own HMO as a competitive alternative. How could they gain the same efficiencies of this model? How could these new HMOs compete in a market like North East Ohio, so overpopulated with health care specialists and doctors?

The idea of a network HMO with a centralized system essentially provided a subset of doctors in one area. These doctors agreed to any and all details of providing care from the fee schedule they established. Basically, the doctor experts debated the techniques and procedures of the delivery of the care well in advance. The byproduct thereafter was an overload of information. All of this data just waiting to be controlled.

Let's remember most of this data I'm talking about was still analog. In other words, it was written down. Like long reports for a school paper, doctors sometimes read thousands of words just to make one decision. Patient records and journal articles were being generated by doctors every day all across the USA. It would take years, maybe even decades, for a diligent system to purpose all this information. This system would need to catch up, if you will. However, many doctors would not wait to see how computers and data collection were going to change their careers. In the early 1980s, individual practitioners, and better yet, a large concerned group of practitioners, banded together and formed an HMO called "Group Health Plan of Northeast Ohio," a 501(c)(3) nonprofit organization with Maxwell Davis as Chairman and Gary Gordon as COO. That's when our man, Michael Keresman, steps into the story.

Gary Gordon enjoyed the glowing accolades and job performance reviews Michael received at Babcock & Wilcox, a well-known construction industry consortium. Mr. Gordon hired Michael with a sizable pay increase that the construction industry could not afford. Please note, Michael had no less than four promotions in two years, demonstrating his cost-cutting controller skills while at Babcock & Wilcox. Gary could see Michael venerated the power of numbers and was eager to see if he could repeat those events with Group Health Plan of Northeast Ohio.

Michael soon learned the business character of Group Health Plan of Northeast Ohio was similar to all the other major medical HMOs: One building meant only one asset to oversee. The lab was on the third floor, the X-ray on the second floor, etc. No tertiary care or sophisticated surgeries were performed.

At the time, critics pointed out that America's old health care system, pre 1960s, was the greatest "sick-care system" in the world. "Once you get sick, it takes care of you." The idea behind Group Health Plan of Northeast Ohio's HMO was in direct response to this criticism. Health maintenance organizations were to take care of you *from the beginning*, before a problem emerged. The notion of annual physicals, routine checkups, regular pap smears, and other systematic visits was born out of this new managed care system. Treating the healthy was a radical concept. Health care was on its way to becoming proactive, rather than reactive.

This cultural shift in the delivery of health care was utterly contrary to mainstream thinking at the time. However, its wisdom was beginning to permeate the American psyche. The public began to shed the idea of seeing a doctor only when they were feeling sick.

Essentially, Michael went to work in the health care industry with the mindset of challenging the status quo!

He was working for a company that was bucking the system from the inside out. Unfortunately, that's when health care costs began to increase.

Principally, we had a cost-plus-health care based system. Michael realized whatever the cost, a profit margin was added on top. Let's use childbirth as an example of the leading trend that needed to be overhauled. It used to be quite common, in the late 1950s and well into the early 1970s, for a woman delivering a baby to stay in the hospital for three-plus days after delivery, sometimes even longer. This concept was completely unheard of before, and completely unheard of ever since. Of course, today holistic care data has proven a contrary perspective: We really ought not be in the hospital more than is absolutely necessary. Psychologically, spiritually, and physically, we have proven patients are better off in their own comfortable environment at home. The hospitals should be for in-depth emergency observation and intensive critical care *only*. But we must remember this is still the 1980s. The world wasn't yet ready for this balanced level of care.

It's important to note that Group Health Plan of Northeast Ohio primarily focused on the lower end of the socioeconomic scale. The care was believed to be every bit as good as nearly all the other programs available because the company adopted more of a civil-activist trajectory, which was remarkably progressive for that time. The marketing and sales teams focused on those individuals that were not poor enough for Medicaid and those not covered by regular health insurance.

For those who had Blue Cross in the 1980s, a monthly premium of say $150 or $175 was quite common. However, if one chose Group Health Plan of Northeast Ohio, the premium was 20% less on average and without co-pays or deductibles, which traditional insurance plans used to limit the number of routine visits. Frankly, Group Health Plan of Northeast Ohio was one of very few companies that marketed their services to this socioeconomic group. There may have been some restrictions, but the care was predominantly the same. For example, it's 8p.m. and your child has a bit of a fever, so you rush him to the hospital emergency room. This visit would be covered by Blue Cross, however, it was not covered by Group Health Plan of Northeastern Ohio. While you *could* go to the ER, your coverage did not include emergency room visits for a malady considered routine or non-life threatening. Your family physician would know that Little Johnny gets a fever three times a year, thus making this visit a routine procedure. Every time you rushed to an emergency room, there was a sizable variance in costs compared to regular office visits. It makes perfect sense today, but back then to those not analyzing the costs of delivery, it really didn't seem like a big deal whatsoever. However, analyzing the costs was Michael's job.

As one might suspect, this new responsibility for the patients, regarding their active involvement in personalized medicine, took a great deal of time to take hold. Thus, began the trend to "self-triage." As an example, the difference between a family physician seeing Johnny for a bump on his head and a neurosurgeon seeing Johnny for a bump on his head can be extreme. A family physician sees a million bumps on the head, and, if he or she is a decent physician, he or she knows what to do. The neurosurgeon, however, tends to see patients with bumps on their heads from a different perspective. First and foremost, bumps are actually "lumps." And lumps on the head may indicate something more critical. This specialist begins the treatment plan differently, perhaps wondering, "Might this be a tumor?" Then the physician moves backward from there.

In short, that's predominantly the mindset and mission for this emerging healthcare industry. Progressive and unique ideas were important, but business efficiencies were paramount. Michael was dared to confront the status quo. Michael realized, "They will listen to any idea if it costs less and delivers a marginally superior product. That's just good business."

Well, after a few weeks with the computer, Michael reckoned, "Now I have an understanding of the capabilities of the PC, I need more time." In fact, Michael needed lots of time. Among other ideas he desperately wanted to develop efficiency models for his company. After several weeks of "playing" with the computer in the office, Michael was granted permission to borrow the computer as he wished. That was the word he used—playing. Michael began to delegate all the work possible within his authority. Because Michael's work needed to be maintained with a high degree of excellence, he assigned pending and needing review work first. Then and only then, he would devote the rest of his day to his new little friend! He even gave *her* a name, "Maud" after Maud Adams. She was an actress made famous in two James Bond movies. This seemed a fitting name at the time, as both were smart and villainous at the beginning. However, Keresman, like Bond, turned his villain to become an asset for the good of Her Majesty's Secret Service. And just like Bond, Michael would frequently work well into the night, learning all he could. This is when his genius stepped in. Michael thought, "This is obviously where all business plans will be constructed in the future. I guess it's time for me to make my first 'computer'" HMO business plan."

Michael did exactly that. Completely on his own volition and on his own time, away from the office, Michael began making a business plan. A month later, he created his first "macro program." It was an elaborate business plan for Group Health Plan of Northeast Ohio. Realizing the limitations of the computing capability back then was more trial and error due to computer memory. Large business plans had to be broken into small pieces, and complicated spreadsheets often caused intense slowdowns, even computer crashes. It was here that everything began to change for Michael. The limitation on computing power needed creative solutions.

Innovatively, Michael found a way to link many small spreadsheets together. Limitations in computer memory actually caused Michael to innovate. Therefore, Michael created as many as 200 "minispreadsheets" with very detailed information that could be linked automatically to the classic financial and analytical statements. The art was activating a "macro-command" that would automatically assemble the spreadsheets in a precise order for the information summary. Referencing an individual box or cell across five or six much larger spreadsheets became a powerful tool, and Michael knew it. Michael didn't realize it at the time, but he was actually "computer programming." Michael would bring up spreadsheet A-1, take the number from this cell and put it in spreadsheet B-1. Then he would bring up spreadsheet B-1, take the result of that and put it in C-1, and so forth and so on. In just a few weeks he actually created a macro that took about a half-hour to execute.

Think of it: in less than three months, Michael went from total computer ignorance to authoring a business plan on a PC! Oh, and it was a macro spreadsheet? A multi-tier spreadsheet?! Funny, but Michael's first spreadsheet was stored on multiple floppy discs!

Group Health Plan of Northeast Ohio joined or merged in with a much larger organization known as HealthAmerica. At first, Michael didn't know any of his accountant peers inside this much larger organization. Michael wondered if they created business plans manually like he was trained in college. Michael recalled how he had to go back over these oversized green sheets, erasing and restarting again and again. It was tedious and time-consuming. As more accurate research was submitted or any small change occurred, it may have taken him two or three days to recalculate the whole spreadsheet by hand. Yes, you read that correctly, two or three days to do all the calculations over again by hand!

Now Michael looked over his computer program work. Did he have a very clean and well-structured business plan? Yep. Did he have accurate assumptions for costs and expenses, etc.? Yes, again. Did he have nifty percentage calculations that would scale appropriately? You bet! He even made sure it looked aesthetically pleasing when copied on a copier machine! Was Michael pleased with his work or proud of his effort? No. No? What is happening? Actually, the next morning Michael was going over his work and an intense sadness, almost a trepidation came over him. Why wasn't he happy? This was innovative and flawless work. It was beautifully presented and somewhat easy to follow. Yet these were not the reasons for his unhappiness. Michael was unhappy because he assumed he was behind all the other accountants inside his organization. He believed that all of his peers in the HealthAmerica already knew all this computer stuff! So, where did this feeling of insecurity come from?

Michael remained resolute. It was really cool that he could make a business plan on Lotus 1-2-3. He was convinced that, given nothing else, he could format a spreadsheet that looked intelligent.

This was a radical advancement away from the wide, manual accounting paper with green bars. Plus, he had to figure out how to shrink the ledger to fit dimensions of an 8.5x11 piece of paper. There was a great deal of creative thinking Michael delivered in making his documents look worthy.

Michael knew Gary Gordon was a zealot for appearance. He preached, "I don't care what you're doing, it must look professional!" From that day forward, Michael made sure every spreadsheet had titles, formatting, and consistent margins. Gary Gordon trained his young protege, "It's all about presentation. If it looks good, it's far more credible. People will read it and believe you, even if you're less precise. If it looks sloppy, you lose your audience." Neatness, appearance, and presentation were paramount in Mr. Gordon's mind.

Gary Gordon may have drilled home the importance of presentation, but Michael took everything from there and made it even better.

Michael had a secret. There was method to his madness. Michael was schooled in the art of flowcharts!

Michael loves to solve puzzles and flowcharts do just that. In essence, flowchart logic is binary. Flowchart theory inherently forces the designer to think with binary outcomes, similar to binary code. Because of the limiting power of 1-2-3 and the low memory available in those days, Michael began drawing a flowchart on a white board, a manual flowchart. Let's say a business plan was 50 pages. Add all of these sub-assumptions and categories and a handful of calculations that factor into spreadsheet A-1, then spread those results with six new calculations that stream somewhere else; it's one colossal flowchart.

Flowcharts are not just an exercise for the mind. They reprogram the process of analytical thinking itself. The discipline, when repeated again and again, teaches one to "flow out" around and through adversity and misfortune. The end result of flowcharting is a process. There isn't necessarily a theory. There's a desired outcome. Defining the problem, more often than not, establishes the solution.

Did you do step A? Yes. Then, go to B. No? Then divert to A1.

All computers are still, no matter how sophisticated, binary. It's yes/no, no/yes and yes/no. The art of writing a computer program is navigating the yeses and the nos. Often, the fewest number of steps necessary are discovered while doing this exercise. To get to the outcome you desire, you first must understand that everything is, in fact, binary. Michael comments today, that even with artificial intelligence (what he likes to call "semi-intelligent intelligence"), and new advancements of computers, we are a little less binary. Mostly binary or all binary, we are still in a binary world.

From his flowcharts, Michael discovered the first and most powerful question that would forever change the health care and insurance industry. Again, given the prism of time, this sounds so basic. The phrase that all health care coverage currently depends on: "Is 'this' covered or not?" Or, maybe better asked, "is this malady, disease, or condition paid for by your health care plan?" If it is covered, how much will it cost the Group Health Plan of Northeast Ohio to deliver the remedy? It didn't matter if it was a broken arm or blurry vision. Michael could prove exactly how much it was going to cost. And, let's not forget, Michael started each patient at exactly the same place. Then everyone moved through the system to find out if the condition is a serviceable care item or not. These were radical concepts we accept without any deliberation today. Once again, Michael asked and then delivered, how are things supposed to be?

HealthAmerica adopted Michael's business plan and universally sent it across the network. His peers quickly realized they were the ones behind the learning curve. The Wall Street Journal article was indeed prophetic. Every business in America was going to have a PC in the future. And Michael knew it too.

Takeaways:

1. "Flow-out" around and through adversity and misfortune
2. How you define the problem, therein lies your solution
3. It's a binary world—fewest number of steps necessary usually wins the day
4. Refocus fear and trepidation—turn foe into friend
5. Get ready to work after hours

Scene 1: "What Do You Know, Anyway?"

The construction industry has always endured favor-granting amongst the various trades. In fact, it has a name and a formal line item on the accounting ledger. It's called "job site inefficiencies." Michael learned all about these inefficiencies and the elaborate agreements with construction clients after graduating college in 1979. Let's be clear, just about every contingency imaginable has been vetted in the construction world. Heck, we are still studying the construction process for world famous and ancient pyramids, roads, walls and even sporting arenas like the Roman Colosseum for clues concerning inefficiencies. Actually, most people enduring a large-scale construction project accept these inefficiencies as just part of the cost of doing business. They know it's the kind of stuff that will be forgotten soon after the project is over. For instance, a percentage of the labor for the plumbers could be surcharged to the client should overtime be necessary for any phase of the job for that week. These are not exact in any way, hence the reason a percentage is used for that cost. The theory is that additional construction management would be necessary if overtime work is assigned. The client needs to pay for that management as a percentage of the total labor cost.

Michael was hired by Babcock & Wilcox right out of college. This was a well-respected, nationally known company that specialized in building power generation equipment, factories or plants, and the complex equipment therein. Basically, upper management was conducting an experiment and Michael Keresman was the guinea pig. They wished to upgrade the sophistication and technical capabilities on their job sites by bringing in college graduates. Let's remember, traditional apprenticeships, or as my father used to call them, "the school of hard knocks," were slowly being replaced with individuals with more formal educations. Back in the 1960s and 1970s, college grads with highly specialized education in accounting and engineering could find work almost instantly upon graduation. However, not everybody was thrilled with a slick, know-it-all college kid showing up on a rough and tumble construction site. In fact, Michael's understanding of the construction industry was next to nothing. That's when he was told by the field manager to just stay out of the way. So that's what Michael did—for a while.

Today Keresman points out, "What are college kids good at? Reading books and writing reports! So, that's exactly how I passed my time in the construction trailer." Note that his real job was to calculate and record various expenses and provide all payroll calculations and service to the 250-man operation. These tasks were completed rapidly, so he began to use his free time reading other material in the trailer. Michael read the boring stuff, which no one wanted to read. Basically, anything lying around was fair game. "Actually, you would be surprised," Keresman points out today, "Union rules, regulations and job descriptions are quite interesting!" Inevitably, Michael's little readings and knowledge proved very valuable.

Disputes are common among the trades. Well, one day, a rather lengthy dispute was raging between two critical unions. They needed a resolution, and they wound up in the job trailer with the Job Superintendent (JS), the highest-ranking manager on the job site. Now to be fair, the field JS had many responsibilities. Rendering a labor solution was not uncommon. Mostly, the buck would be passed back to the foremen. The JS would much rather they work it out amongst themselves. However, these men were not backing down. They wanted a solution from the JS himself. Michael listened from the far end of the trailer. Seemingly not even involved in the conversation, Michael quietly gathered their testimony. He wrote the facts down as they made their pleas. Upon judgment by the JS manager, Michael spoke up in contrast to the reckoning. Confidently, Michael laid out his understanding of the union rules, regulations and job descriptions for all concerned. "What do you know, anyway? You're just a dumb college kid." was the response from the JS manager. The union representatives were flummoxed to say the least. So, Michael found the union hand-book on the spot. He openly quoted from the book exactly as he stated a moment earlier. All were amazed!

Over the next few months, Michael became "the expert" in two ways: first as a the "judge" and then as the "arbitrator" for many union disputes. Mr. Keresman went on to say, "In the end, people take pride in their skills. I wanted to create an environment and the opportunity for the skilled laborers to exercise their craft." Word got around fast. Michael had no fewer than four promotions in two years while at Babcock & Wilcox.

CHAPTER 2

Praise Pricklies & The Plaza

Adversity, when properly channeled, will buy you a
ticket to a place you could never have gone before.

Michael always appreciated what his mother Miriam did for him. Sacrifices made by mothers usually go unnoticed by their sons and daughters until much later in life, usually when they have children of their own. However, now that Michael was living alone, he would frequently pop over for Sunday night supper to thank her once again for being such a wonderful mom. Actually, Michael always thought of his mother as being larger than life. In a way, he would always look up to her.

In physical stature, Michael's growth was mainly in his sophomore year at John Carroll University. In that year, Michael topped out at nearly 6 feet, 3 inches tall. Miriam was tall for a woman, and slender too. People would say that Michael took after his mother. Michael has dark olive skin, and he's handsome and well groomed. Michael looks and acts authoritatively. Miriam taught him to be this way. However, Michael's power physically is usually underestimated. It demonstrates something hard to recognize otherwise; this "something"—high physical energy and strength, commonly found in many successful entrepreneurs.

The first person to recognize Michael's uncanny physical strength given his stature at the time was the Normandy High School football coach. As mentioned, the growth spurt so common for boys in high school had not kicked in for Michael. Frankly, all the way through high school Michael was small. However, as Michael's younger brother Matt once commented, "No one on the football field hit more effectively than Mike." Coach Walt Armor once told Michael's father that if he had a full team of players exactly like his son, a state championship berth would be likely. Coach Armor thought the compliment would be received well by the elder Keresman. It wasn't. His father, unfortunately at the time, did not detect the distinction being made about his eldest son's abilities. In fact, Michael's father needed to set the record straight. Matt was going to be the real football star of the family! Actually, Coach Armor believed of all his players on that high school football team, physically, mentally or even passionately, Michael played at a different level. Some people call this focus. In the preface I mentioned that Michael's not like us. However, physically is not what I mean when I say, "he's not like us." Regardless, the distinction here—Michael's focus—especially while in a combative situation is truly uncanny.

On one Sunday night visit Miriam noticed that her little boy was now a grown man. She wondered how the years just slipped by. Michael was just sitting there motionless. She caught Michael deep in thought. She always noticed the duality in Michael's demeanor. Michael is usually smiling gregariously or deep in thought. One or the other. Miriam noticed once again, when deep in thought, his face was completely still. Every muscle was without tension. He appeared like a statue just sitting there alone in the room. However, when his attention is diverted to anyone, it is in fact, his full attention. And that's when it happens. Michael will say your name, and sometimes your full Christian and surname to boot. Frankly, it's a pleasure because Michael is endowed with a beautiful speaking voice. It is deep and syrupy. Miriam always adored how he used his whole body to resonate all kinds of tones when he spoke. Basically, when Michael talks, you just want to listen. However, when Miriam would catch Michael in one of these solitude moments, she enjoyed surprising him. It was just a little game she played. Michael carried on this unusual tradition today. The sudden unexpected popup, "What are you doing?" usually jolts anyone awake. This was one of those occasions when Miriam came to see her son on the porch. Michael was deep in contemplation. Something or someone was unquestionably on his mind. Miriam burst onto the porch and with full voice, "MICHAEL KERESMAN!" She then paused to see if she would get a reaction. Michael was used to her antics; he didn't move. Miriam continued, "You know Michael, my big-shot executive son, it has been awhile since I've seen you in a new business suit." Michael slowly drew his attention towards her. He thought, what is she up to now? Michael knew things were truly different. Everything seemed a little odd. However, he truly enjoyed being on his own, taking care of himself.

She continued, "I was just in the mall the other day, and I saw some very handsome suits for 35% off. We've shopped there before, over at Pierre Gordon's. We should get you back there. Maybe we can find a nice new suit." Michael thought the last thing he wants to do right now is go shopping with his mother!

"Ma, I'm a grown man, I can buy my own clothes." Miriam would have none of it. Miriam raised four children, helped pay their way through school, and earned a Ph.D. in psychology well after marriage and children. "Well, fine. Then you can take me to lunch, now that you are a big shot executive at HealthAmerica!"

Michael protested "MA!" Then he paused for just a second and saw something distinctive, his beloved mother's smile. The smile that radiated from her soul. The smile that glistened through her bright blue eyes. Michael continued, "Actually, I need to tell you something. I'm up for a promotion." Michael remained motionless, he wanted to see her face again. He continued, "but I think I'm going to resign from HealthAmerica instead. Yes Ma, your son is a quitter!" She did not laugh. Instead Miriam sat down next to her son. Her face was calm and relaxed. She was more than willing to listen to more. Michael continued, "There is a group of scientists, executives and entrepreneurs coming together to form a company up in Mentor. They have created some sterilization solutions and processes for the medical world. And I think they just asked me to be a co-founder." Michael stopped talking. He glanced outside at the rusty old swing set in the back yard. Miriam knew her son. She knew to stay silent. She said nothing. She just warmly smiled. When Michael looked back, she tilted her head slightly. Michael continued, "Bill Sanford, a brilliant and experienced executive, just moved up here from Columbus. He was looking to find someone to accept his rigorous standards. Mr. Sanford claimed I was exactly the match he wanted. He says he needs someone curious and hardworking, with a need to learn from the best." Repeating that phrase made him laugh a little.

Miriam looked at her son as if to say, 'good for you son.' That's when it happened. At that very second Michael knew he was going shopping with his mother. Oh, she was good all right, and, more than likely he would end up buying lunch, too! The truth was, Michael knew his mother was proud of him. Michael wanted to thank her in some way. So, he thought, why not let her be a mom one last time. Michael smiled back. That's all she needed. Miriam piped up, "Perfect! If that's the case, you're going to take this new job, and you're really going to need a new suit." Michael thought, she's right. He does need a new suit. Miriam continued, "And if the suit doesn't look good on you, who's going to let you know? The salesman?" Miriam had a point. They both laughed. The true master negotiator had spoken!

Just an aside here: Malachi Mixon, another influential Cleveland entrepreneur, had focused on Bill Sanford for this opening and the building of STERIS. Ironically, both Mixon and Sanford were originally from humble beginnings in Missouri. Frankly, the two men were using their investor relationship with Primus Capital to help Cleveland with growth opportunities. That's when Michael Keresman stepped into this story.

So, Michael picked up his mother at exactly 11 a.m. the next day. Their destination was the largest mall in the United States at that time, Randall Park Mall. There, in a crowded and well-integrated suburb of Cleveland, Ohio, Michael would use his brand-new Visa Credit Card to buy a charcoal grey, three-piece suit that Miriam helped him pick out! The cost was $89.50. That was a good deal! Two weeks later Michael glided into his new place of work, STERIS Corporation, looking like a million bucks. It was 1987.

A decade later in 1997, Bill Sanford and Michael Keresman, CEO and CFO of STERIS, could afford the finest hand tailored suits directly from Italy. Their remarkable hard work and great fortune led to unprecedented growth and development of Cleveland's new darling corporation. The men were proud, and for good reason. Their relentless work ethic served as an impetus for each other and as an example to the rest of their peers and underlings at STERIS. During that decade it was not unusual for each of them to stay late two or three times a week. It was another psychological game they played, almost challenging the other for the honor of being the last man out. With that kind of rivalry and camaraderie, the men became very close indeed.

Let's not forget that this all came together under the leadership of Bill Sanford. Eventually, Michael earned Bill's ear, as they say. Plus, Michael made sure their interpersonal relationship was on a different level than all the other employees. Michael was a slave to brokering power. Make no mistake, Michael made sure Sanford's authority was secured first. Then, he would enhance his own image and ambitions thereafter. One long-time ex-employee observed, "That kind of trust and respect is so rare. But I got to see these men interact every week. It was amazing." Many people believe STERIS's mission remains successful today because of the Sanford and Keresman team established in the 1990s.

Here is the STERIS mission statement: To help customers create a healthier and safer world by providing innovative healthcare and life science product and service solutions around the globe.

In the mid 1990s, STERIS had become the leading provider of infection prevention and surgical support. STERIS focused primarily on the health care, pharmaceutical and medical device industries. Michael and Bill had set up the core competencies of the company. Back then, and still to this day, STERIS offered a mix of innovative capital equipment and supply products, such as: sterilizers and washers, surgical tables, lights, and equipment management systems. Bill Sanford made sure that the connectivity solutions followed the products into every sales opportunity, including operating room integration, consumable products like sterilant, detergents, gastrointestinal endoscopy accessories, and other products and services. Service was not service if it did not include equipment installation and maintenance, microbial reduction of medical devices, instrument and scope repairs, plus labo-ratory services and off-site reprocessing.

Bill Sanford had the vision, polish and personality and Michael had the accounting acumen to be an ideal complement. A bond forged from this unrelenting competitive spirit can be defined in one word, accountability. Mediocrity was the enemy! Praise and pricklies rolled off their tongues toward one another in every conversation. The result was a well-polished Bill Sanford who could glide onto any stage he wished, just as if he was picking up his third Oscar at the Academy Awards. For Bill Sanford, each performance was more refined than the last. As for Michael, the sharpness of his mind could only be compared to that of a ninja warrior; precisely what Bill needed by his side.

Crain's Cleveland Business, a weekly newspaper that reported important business dealings of northeast Ohio, would often solicit both men for comments on the stories featured on STERIS. The two men provided an interdependent yin and yang for their company and, more importantly, for each other.

As a result, Sanford found himself thinking out loud in Michael's presence. Michael filed away many of these thoughts and concerns. Michael instinctively knew these little utterances would be helpful to not only Sanford but ultimately to STERIS itself. One Sanford irritant was the brain-drain at STERIS. Sanford was livid that other compa-nies filched some of their best employees. This is a double edge sword. Attracting the best employees means you may need to replace them from time to time.

All businesses need to replace their labor force. Negative effects in productivity are common. As Mr. Keresman once said, "The bottom line is always under assault!" In times of wealth expansion, labor becomes scarce and expensive. Eventually, highly skilled labor becomes very expensive. This can be traced to the fundamental forces of capitalism itself, as the marketplace for excellence is constantly challenged and then re-challenged to establish an equilibrium. Generally, all busi-nesses quantify the losses for replacements in their annual reports. However, for STERIS things were a little different.

Once Michael was put in charge by Sanford, he found a way to place STERIS at the top for employee retention. Michael realized three key aspects for any business can be found in human resourcing. The first being that it was far more efficient to find ways to keep the best people. This includes getting to know each employee's needs, wants and desires. Second, it was equally beneficial to allow the weaker performers to "slip out the back door." And third, that shaping each division of the business was like setting up a chess board so that all the variety of pieces from pawns to knights and bishops to queen must work together to defend the king. Interestingly, Michael built his chess board managing his losses or sacrifices with a super goal in mind: to put the other guy in check.

"Unbeknownst to the rest of the world, Cleveland is a wonderful place to live. Raising a family is quite comfortable here!" Mr. Keresman went on to say, "The list of positives in Cleveland far outweigh the negatives represented by others outside our area." This was a mindset. Frankly, Michael's unrelenting sales and PR to his management and staff ended the brain drain for STERIS. Plus, he exhibited appreciation for his Cleveland heritage every single day. Michael would point out that Cleveland consistently performs well in overall ratings for quality of life. If Michael was pressed to compare Cleveland to a big market like Chicago, New York, Philadelphia or LA, it was a no brainer. The exorbitant cost for a comparable quality of life in any of these cities was simply stifling.

Here are a few other examples Michael would spin. The Cleveland professional sports teams have regularly contended for national titles in football, baseball, and basketball since the early 1900s. The arts, such as The Cleveland Orchestra, Cleveland Art Museum, and Playhouse Square, attract world renowned talent annually. Then there are comedy clubs, an innovative bar scene, and foodies like Michael Symon, Doug Katz and Zack Bruell. Cleveland is home to The Rock & Roll Hall of Fame as well. There is a beautiful Great Lake, Lake Erie, on the northern border. For boaters, sailors, fishermen, hunters and beachgoers, endless adventures can be found. We have the John Glenn NASA Research Center. We have the annual Cleveland National Air Show with the likes of the Blue Angels and Thunderbirds. Cleveland has world famous architecture, great neighborhoods, and a diverse population that gets along pretty darn well. The public schools are good and there are numerous private schools, which are more than good at twice the price. Liberal thinkers in businesses and education are consistently tempered with conservative values to meld our pot of gold under a glorious rainbow!

From an employee retention perspective, there is no wisdom in uprooting a family from such a wonderful place! Enthusiasm and pride for Cleveland was not just a selling slogan from Michael, it was a goal he had from his childhood. Both the city and man have a chip on their shoulders. Both have always felt they had something to prove to the world. I'm certain Michael knew this consciously throughout his adult life. The last thing he was going to do was fall short of one of his goals! And Cleveland was going to come along for the ride.

In Michael's business world at STERIS, he found that the vast majority of the workforce could be placed in one of two categories; employees are either articulates or competents. Stopping here for just a moment, this seems very straightforward. If you can speak authoritatively with in-depth insight and accuracy, you are considered articulate. If not, then you may be a poor communicator and inarticulate. Also, if you do your job really well with few or no mistakes, then you are competent. If not, then you are less competent. However, here is what Michael noticed next. At STERIS he had plenty of truly remarkable and talented people that simply could not talk or write with any authority about their research or work. But they did their job really well! And of course, Michael noticed the opposite. At STERIS he had a few employees that knew everything there was to know about the product or processes they market at STERIS. These individuals could lecture all day and others would gladly listen to every word. These people have a knack for explaining complex ideas clearly. However, sometimes when these people are asked to take a project from beginning to end, they became confused and completely lost. In this way, Michael encouraged the articulates into sales, training and customer service while moving the competents into research, development and system analysis.

Perhaps you are thinking, what about someone who is just average at both? Do they have a place in the system? Of course, Michael says, "That's really most of the world anyway." However, Michael incessantly searched for the high positives! He did not want to lose these individuals. But what about those who have high positives in both categories? Michael says, "These are rare souls indeed." He called them the competent articulates. Michael claims, "these gems cannot be replaced, hang onto them at all costs." Michael kept a mental scale from 10 to 1 for all his employees. From High Articulates to low or inarticulate and High Competents to low or incompetent, Michael knew the rarest of all could be found—The High Competent and High Articulate.

Michael's first priority was to elevate his low performers to competent contributors. In this way, he and Sanford would generate loyalty and pride in STERIS. The next lesson Michael learned was how to slide the weaker performers, the total incompetents, towards the door. Setting up a billion-dollar business is going to get messy at times, especially where humans are involved. Again, it almost always comes down to accountability, relentless accountability. Michael cautions entrepreneurs today, "Be on the lookout for those individuals that provide minimal activity while maintaining observable professional decorum." Here Michael would compassionately explain their weaknesses in person; never allowing himself the pettiness to suggest any limitations he witnessed behind their back. Realizing the "reality of the situation," people would invariably do the right thing and move on to a better fit elsewhere.

Bill Sanford and Michael Keresman were very much like the heads of the family. As father and mother, so to speak, they educated, shepherded, and fostered hundreds of associates and employees over the years. One of those young associates was an intern named Tim Sherwin.

Tim's father, a well-known businessman from the famous Sherwin family of Sherwin-Williams, let his son know that he should not expect any privileges because of family money and name. Now that Tim had graduated from college, he encouraged his son to find a job all by himself. So, Tim set out to prove something, and prove something he did. Tim was a handsome, athletic youth with social skills to rival Miss Manners. He had quick wit, a wry smile. Tim could handle just about anyone and anything with ease. Tim wanted something more in his career, and his internship at STERIS was the first place he looked.

Born in the 1970s, a small segment of Tim's generation fits neatly into the "renaissance-man" type. Tim Sherwin is part of that segment. In fact, I believe Tim represents the luckiest generation to ever come along the human timeline. In general, they are old enough to have learned valuable life lessons from the "Great Generation." In addition, they are just young enough to have flipped on a PC before leaving high school or college. They watched and participated in the era of significant growth and prosperity in the 1980s and 1990s, known as the Reagan Era. There were no anti-war, anti-America protests. No social media distractions. No helicopter parents to battle. Basically, they were raised and encouraged in the greatest of all disciplines, individualism! In addition, and perhaps their most profound opportunity and accomplishment, they were the first generation to write, create, and manipulate software! It really didn't matter how good it was, either. They learned the process! They created the flowcharts from scratch. Productivity and control on multiple levels was never more streamlined in history. They expected great things from one another. Plus, the advent of the internet was just beginning. Everyone knew the train was coming fast, especially Tim Sherwin. He was going to make sure he was on that train. Not as a passenger either, but he made sure he was out front by the power, the engine. Tim was comfortable around dominant people. Tim was aspiring to be the train's engineer. However, if that meant shoveling coal into the furnace, for now, that would be fine. Michael saw all this and never took his eye off the young man. Michael instinctively knew he could cultivate even more than Tim imagined in himself. Tim was an eager intern in the summer of 1993 when he started with STERIS. Michael had instantly placed Tim in the "High Competent and High Articulate" column, the rarest of all individuals in business. Michael saw something familiar here. Michael didn't know it then, but Tim would later go on to be a critical member and cofounder of CardinalCommerce. Either way Michael, knew not to lose track of Tim Sherwin.

The Plaza

In 1998 Michael Keresman began to feel the sensation of wanting to be his own boss. He wanted to explore what it would be like to start a business from scratch. He was confident and ready. He even had the name "Cardinal" from a reoccurring dream. Frankly, there wasn't much else to go on; it was just a name from a dream. Michael was a high-power executive with STERIS, but he wanted more. Bill Sanford had done everything he could for Michael and Michael had done everything he could for Bill and STERIS. Michael built everything by putting numbers in boxes. Wall Street loved guys like Michael because his numbers were solid. They could trust Michael. If anything, Michael was too conservative. Michael had a sharp blade alright, and Sanford knew exactly how to use it. And now it was clear, a showdown between the two men may be unavoidable. All the power structures inside this billion-dollar business flowed directly thru one of these two men. Instinctively, Michael understood one way or the other the power could no longer be shared in this way. He anticipated that the executive board of STERIS was willing to exercise its control over the two men. Interestingly, neither Bill nor Michael could stand the thought of a STERIS without the other. Michael was in a pickle and it was weighing heavy on his heart.

However, being an executive of a billion-dollar business can have some rather interesting perks. Rubbing elbows with really clever entrepreneurs is one of them. In so doing, Michael was taking notice of how merchants and banks viewed the internet as a new cost-effective sales opportunity. Merchants began to anticipate a future with lower infrastructure costs, i.e. fewer buildings and storefronts. Banks saw the opportunity to convert costly paper-based-payments (i.e. cash/checks) which represented 75% of all payments to revenue generating credit card payments. However, Michael noticed e-commerce was riddled with fraud and vulnerability. Consumers were always validated by the merchant at the point of sale. The payment industry was specifically designed for face-to-face commerce. Verification was dependent upon the consumer presenting a credit card and a signature to an individual at a known location. Most often, additional forms of identification were presented for added security.

Michael noticed, from a consumer's perspective, this was a simple unobtrusive process that worked extremely well. For merchants and issuing banks, this process cleanly facilitated the selling of goods and services. However, the system that was both effective and efficient in the face-to-face world had its challenges on the internet. Michael began to think once again, "how is this world supposed to be."

Actually, to ensure e-commerce growth, Visa and Mastercard developed programs—Verified by Visa and MasterCard Secure Code—which endeavored to eliminate fraud. Frankly, many industry insiders didn't believe these programs worked all that well. These programs required issuing banks to positively identify their customers during an internet transaction. That's a good thing, however the greatest effect of this change was that fraud-loss liability shifted from merchants to financial institutions. That's a bad thing. As a result, issuing banks needed authentication services to avoid absorbing the $60 billion annually in fraud losses projected for the new millennial era. Think of it—the dawn of the new millennial era and internet fraud was draining the system by billions and billions of dollars. Michael had no idea about any of these numbers. Michael had much more important matters at hand. It was December 1998. The construction of his new house was not finished, and Michael needed to get Bill and STERIS off his mind for a while. But most importantly, Michael was determined to not be the "Grinch" that stole Christmas.

Too often, in our highly competitive world, certain executives wrestle the intense pressures of entrepreneurship against family life. It's easy to feel like the loner, or the Grinch when this happens. But Michael had a new idea for this holiday season: "Let's take the whole family away for a change." Now, could he and his wife, Liz, find the right place to create some Christmas wonder for their girls? Liz remembered, "The house in Mentor was in no shape for a proper Christmas for our young ladies." Liz also recalls wanting to give Josie, their youngest daughter, only 4 at the time, a magical Christmas. Liz said, "She loved the book 'Eloise at The Plaza,' plus daughters Katie and Jackie watched the hit movie 'Home Alone 2: Lost in New York' over and over." That's it! The Keresmans were going to the Big Apple, for a wonderful Christmas vacation at The Plaza Hotel. Both the book and movie utilized The Plaza Hotel as a major setting and focal point. One way or another, this is going to be the most memorable Christmas in Keresman history.

Actually, what happens in real-life parallels the fanciful Hollywood film, "Home Alone 2." It is hard to fathom as one looks back on the excess influences that change one's life. However, on that family vacation, Michael unwittingly became his own version of the character Kevin McCallister. This is exactly how CardinalCommerce, one of the most influential software companies for e-commerce, was forged into being.

Now settled in at the Plaza, the family was especially focused on

4½-year-old Josie, Michael and Liz's youngest daughter. Somehow, Josie was distracted when a Christmas tree and brightly wrapped presents were delivered and set into place in the parents' adjacent room. The evening went off without a hitch. Josie was completely unawares. After putting the girls down to bed, Liz wanted a warm bath and comfy bed; and Michael, a night cap and cigarette. At nearly midnight on Christmas Eve, I find it rather remarkable that anyone could go to the bar at The Plaza Hotel and find inspiration for a future groundbreaking software company. But that's exactly what happened to Michael Keresman in 1998.

As it turned out, there were two businessmen also there at the bar. Just like "Home Alone 2's" Harry and Marv, they were plotting their future, or should we say their next heist, too. Michael listened in. Their "concept in development" was to build out a free internet service provider company and then make a quick sell. Of course, their plan was, in actuality, more of a get-rich-quick scam. However, Michael saw right through the smoke screen to the value side of their proposition and ploy. Michael began to think about the World Wide Web and where it may go in the future. After all, cutting edge internet commerce was yet to be fully developed.

Anyone who has been groomed for business as Michael had could easily sense everything was about to change because of the internet. Well, the drinks flowed for over three hours, and as he listened to how the internet was quickly evolving and its potential, he knew there was a place for him, too. The more they talked, the more Michael realized that the public was vulnerable and needed protection, some way to make the internet safe and secure. Wait just a minute:

Did Michael just find the impetus to leave STERIS?

Could Michael even build an internet software team?

Would Cleveland even support such a cutting-edge enterprise?

Could he even afford ramping up a software upstart?

Would his peers in the business community think he's off his rocker?

And most importantly, would Bill Sanford thwart his leaving of STERIS?

Well, one thing was certain. Michael had a dream, a dream of building something "the way it's supposed to be." Perhaps this is it. Actually, the answers to all these questions didn't take very long for Michael, maybe two or three months. Plus, in Michael's mind, he could easily secure Cardinal's first employee, Tim Sherwin. And completely unbeknownst to Michael, Tim was cultivating a friendship and business relationship with a really clever and talkative technology writer in Detroit. His name is Chandra. I wonder, would Michael appraise Chandra as a competent or an articulate? To Tim, Chandra was a no brainer!

Takeaways:

1. Broker power for your boss: learn what he or she needs
2. Delegate authority—employees move like chess pieces
3. Always be a cheerleader for your hometown / business
4. Listen, listen, listen. How are things supposed to be?
5. Don't be the Grinch

Scene 2: "The Bluff"

After Bill Sanford and Michael Keresman successfully launched STERIS on the Nasdaq stock exchange, they began to look for new opportunities, not for themselves, per se, but for STERIS.

Michael noted that "from a position of power, all things are possible in business and in war." This postulate is from "Marketing Warfare" by Al Ries and Jack Trout, a favorite book of Michael's. Marketing campaigns are drawn from the similarities found in the basic forms of warfare: defend, attack, flank attack, and guerilla.

Plus, STERIS, for reasons which included mostly Michael Keresman, had an immaculate Wall Street reputation. Bill understood this fact, and he used Michael to help grow the company significantly. Some might say Bill manipulated Michael with loyalty. Michael said, "It was just Bill being Bill. He's a competitive guy, and he pushed me really hard." Michael went on to say, "We have always remained the best of friends. And frankly, I pushed Bill pretty hard too! I don't know what I would have done without Bill."

Frequently, STERIS was being compared to other "like companies" in the health care and medical device sector. This is perhaps Wall Street's favorite pastime: comparing and contrasting peers in all the various sectors of the economy. Inevitably, STERIS was looked upon as the "little brother" of American Sterilizing Company, AMSCO, which was also traded on the Nasdaq. However, at that time, AMSCO had just been downgraded significantly. Apparently, some rogue executives from its North Carolina plant had fudged some patent restrictions. The FDA stepped in and basically slapped them pretty hard. The FDA forbid any new AMSCO product introduction for 18 months. This was not a death sentence, but it meant upper management better get things tidied up soon. That's when Bill swooped in. AMSCO was about five times larger than STERIS, and the deal on Wall Street became "the minnow that swallowed the whale."

I should point out, AMSCO was out of Pittsburgh, Pennsylvania. The Pittsburgh hockey team, the Penguins, won the Stanley Cup in 1991 and 1992. AMSCO, being a supporter of everything Pittsburgh, enjoyed entertaining clients with a luxury suite at the Penguins' arena. In addition, the second favorite pastime of high finance analysts is comparing and contrasting major athletic teams in all the various sectors of the major sports economy. Basically, Wall Street loves rivalries. And, Keresman had a knack for remembering everyone's favorite team.

Well, Bill gambled with his rival and ace in the hole, Michael Keresman. Basically, Bill had a handshake agreement with the FDA. Should STERIS gain control of AMSCO's board and company the FDA would agree to lift any restrictions. That meant Bill and Mike would need to travel all over the USA meeting with hedge fund managers, institutional brokers, and major stock owners of both STERIS and AMSCO to sell the idea that the combined company was synergistically better than two separate companies. Could they convince "the street" that their vision, albeit highly ambitious, was going to work?

The board at AMSCO would not be undersold. They hired their own guy to clean things up, a workout specialist and value investor specialist named Dick Gillian. Those who watch this type of thing know what comes next. Both stocks started to slip in share price as news worked its way out. The stocks weren't affected too significantly, just enough to make things interesting. Each stock slipped by roughly 20% in the weeks that followed.

This was a controversial deal. There was little to no institutional support and almost no analyst coverage to recommend the deal to the multitude of institutional investors. Without recommendations, the deal seemed destined to fail.

Bill and Michael needed to make their pitch directly to their institutional stockholders, or better yet, to sell the merger concept to potential institutional holders who would like the combined company better. Bill and Michael understood that the new stockholders of the merger would have to see this as a truly opportunistic deal. They embarked on a road trip, visiting 15 cities in just 10 days.

Bill pushed Michael out front as much as he could stand. Sharing the limelight was not that easy for Bill. Remember, Bill could light up a room with southern charm to boot. Still, he knew all the Wall Street insiders trusted Michael completely.

Just as they finished another road show presentation on the West Coast, Bill, Michael, and a couple of analysts from McDonald & Company, a Cleveland-based full-service investment firm, learned that the actual showdown may be over. The fellows from McDonald & Company received back channel information that an institutional investor in Chicago was voting against the STERIS takeover. Thousands of stock proxies for both companies, STERIS and AMSCO, were held at one of the largest investment houses in the country. However, Michael recalled talking with this institutional investor in Chicago on a few previous occasions.

The scene actually plays out in the back seat of a limo ride to the airport. Michael remembered that everyone was pretty tired and cranky as they were being picked up for the ride to the private jet airfield. That's when Michael got the bad news from his honchos at McDonald & Co. Michael began to put in the numbers of the acquaintance in Chicago. The McDonald guys went crazy; they tried to stop Michael. That's when Bill jumped in and with a cold stare, he motioned for the McDonald men to stand down. Bill wanted Michael to try his spiel. The man in Chicago (let's call him Benjamin) answered his phone. Please be reminded this is the flip phone era. Only astute, fastidious guys like Michael collected everybody's personal number. That alone is amazing. The conversation went something like this.

MICHAEL: Hi Ben. This is Michael Keresman from STERIS. Hey, incidentally, how are your Blackhawks doing this season? I understand they beat the Penguins the other night.

BENJAMIN: Oh Hi Mike. That's right. It was an epic game! But I'm sure that's not why you are calling me.

MICHAEL: Yes Ben, you're right. I'm calling because I just got word that you may be against the deal we proposed.

Michael remained silent waiting for a response.

BENJAMIN: Well, my clients have watched the stock price fall recently. After your deal falls apart, my clients should see both STERIS and AMSCO stocks return to normalcy. That's when I will most likely dump my clients' interest in both companies.

MICHAEL: Well, aren't you making an assumption?

BENJAMIN: What assumption would that be?

MICHAEL: That we . . . or I should say "management" would stay.

Michael went silent. The pause was long, but Michael was not about to break the moment he just created. Benjamin was obviously weighing Michael's meaning.

BENJAMIN: Whaaa, waaa, what are you . . . what assumption would that be?

Michael took his time. He explained without passion . . .

MICHAEL: This is an important deal for STERIS. Bill and I have put in thousands of hours contemplating *all the ramifications* of adding the AMSCO assets to STERIS. I personally have contingencies for just about everything you can imagine for our future together. But, if you think you can do better running the company without us, then please have at it.

Michael went silent one last time. Benjamin considered his options. The men in the limo were apoplectic with anticipation. Bill held his cold stare. No one said a word. If Michael failed here, it would be all his doing. If he didn't, Bill would be the CEO of a soon-to-be multibillion-dollar company.

BENJAMIN: Michael, you have a deal. I'm going to vote for the STERIS takeover of AMSCO.

MICHAEL: Good decision, Benjamin. You won't be disappointed. I can promise you that. And good luck with the Blackhawks with the remainder of the season. Who knows, it might be against those nasty Penguins?

Both men laughed and said goodbye.

Bill and the others waited for the flip phone to close. Then . . .

The McDonald partners cheered like they won the Stanley Cup!

BILL: Jesus, Mike! "All the contingencies you can imagine?" I would like to see that.

CHAPTER 3

A Banker, The Professor & Everybody's Best Man

When the pupil is ready the master appears.

Sociologists agree ceremonies were created by the keepers of the status quo for the overall survival of the society they helped construct. Consider the thousands of dollars and countless hours spent planning and executing graduations, birthdays, First Communions, Bar Mitzvahs and, of course, everyone's favorite, the wedding ceremony. There is one role at this ceremony that is the envy of all others (and it's not the groom)—the "best man." The title says it all. To stand alongside a friend in a wedding is an honor that many men desire. Frankly, the best man is the affirmation of the most powerful relationship outside the husband and wife.

Well, Michael enjoys rituals and ceremonies just as much as anyone else. And, as stated earlier, Michael is a keen observer of all those around him. Scrutinizing the small interactions of subordinates is essential for anyone training to be a CEO. Michael was doing exactly that while he was at STERIS.

Back in the 1990s, Michael noticed a certain junior account executive who was accumulating a curious statistic well outside the normalcy curve. This odd statistic had nothing to do with conventional business or sales practices. Michael learned about a young man who was well on his way to becoming a groomsman in over a dozen weddings and a best man in three or four more! Undeniably, a unique individual; Michael thought so too. And that role, as best man, is how I would define the relationship between Michael Keresman and Tim Sherwin: Tim was Michael's best man.

I imagine Michael saw the accumulation of Tim's amazing wedding participations as a nod toward one of the essential qualities he might need some day for his new company. Loyalty heads the list. Michael meticulously developed loyalty with Bill Sanford while at STERIS. From Bill Sanford, to Michael Keresman, to Tim Sherwin, we see a gradual progression in leadership development. Succession may not seem that important to most people, but in the game of business, as in "The Game of Thrones," it's nearly everything.

Tim Sherwin wielded his people skills like a sword that singled him out for succession at Cardinal. Tim carried this sword like Excalibur, King Arthur's famous armament. Tim Sherwin is the Boy-King Arthur himself. As the legend is told, "He, Arthur, drew from the stone, Excalibur with ease, what all others could not." The legend then reveals Arthur developed his authority into something way more powerful than a sword.

Those who study leadership venerate these stories. What made Arthur, King Arthur? Was it just his sword, Excalibur, the greatest of all swords? Or was it perhaps something else, something more subtle inside the man that others admire and gravitate toward? I'm talking about the ultimate power necessary in building anything of quality, like a kingdom or its modern-day equivalent: a major company and business.

Most people dismiss, or even forget, one of the most important parts in the Arthurian legend. I'm speaking of Arthur's Round Table. Without it, Arthur would have been the same as any other king. Excalibur may be the sword, but the Round Table is something very different. At the Round Table, all the knights gathered to share stories of unselfish and chivalrous acts they performed across the kingdom. This was for all things good. Arthur believed that his kingdom, Camelot, should be molded on mutual respect and love, not anxiety over royal reprisal. The knights of the Round Table must be the example that will esteem Camelot above all other kingdoms. The Round Table is a metaphor for a new type of leadership: informal authority. I believe Tim may hold a version of this influence, too.

When Tim comes into a room, he earns trust and love from those around him almost immediately, without having to be dictatorial. His connection with the employees and workforce is more empathetic. Tim genuinely troubles himself with the needs of others. Tim pointed out, "It's the way I run Cardinal now." Of course, after the sale of CardinalCommerce to Visa in 2017, Michael's well-deserved retirement made for a timely transition. That's when Tim Sherwin became CEO of CardinalCommerce. "For me, it's all about empowerment and trust," he said. "I think people definitely perform at a way higher level when they care about what they're doing. In general, we are empowered to make decent decisions when we are not fearful of punishment. We learn to face risk, whatever that may be, head on." Cardinal's culture has evolved because of Tim Sherwin. All the employees, either consciously and or subconsciously, let Tim graciously lead CardinalCommerce forward.

At the very beginning in 1999 Michael and Tim cultivated Chandra Balasubramanian to join the fledgling company. It was only a matter of time before Chandra could get out of his contract in Detroit and work his way to Cleveland. To secure Tim and Chandra, Michael offered the young men well-deserved "co-founder" positions. Now the hard part: the details of creating a software, intellectual property, internet services company would be a challenge for sure. Either way, the fledgling company that was soon to become CardinalCommerce was taking form.

The grand differences between Michael and Tim are less important in the scheme of creating something greater than oneself. These men willingly and passionately worked together. Michael's vision and outcomes were well-defined each day, each week, each month, and every year from the very start. This was essential for success at that time. Michael knew he had to be firm and unwavering. In my estimation, the unique blend of Michael's formal authority and Tim's informal authority were fused into the success of CardinalCommerce.

Michael grasped Tim's potential from the very beginning. If Cardinal was to build a relationship with the status quo based on mutual respect, if there was to be a marriage, then everybody knows we need a best man.

Assessing the various shortcomings and the inclusive strengths of your employees is a full-time job for any CEO. However, growing your company together with your employees is another matter entirely.

Michael never tired of either, the assessing or the growing, as his relationship with Chandra Balasubramanian demonstrates.

Chandra Balasubramanian's presence is evident when he enters a room, but not commanding. His height, broad shoulders, and round chest contribute to the appearance of being a big man, yet he moves gently, lyrically. He has a youthful, almost cherub-like face capped with jet black hair. Initial eye contact with Chandra is calming and pleasant, but intriguing at the same time. He has a playful, sometimes mischievous smile and happy demeanor.

Chandra can file away for future use any piece of information he wishes, no matter how innocuous. Chandra acts like a hip college professor. But not just any college professor; he would be the beloved, popular teacher. He would teach the one class everyone wanted to take. Not because it was easy, but because the students know they are going to learn. Chandra wants the best for you. In fact, Chandra believes everybody can be successful at something.

In 1995, just two years before Chandra would move from India to Detroit for his first real employment in the USA, the predominant way to get online was through early service providers like American Online (AOL). However, there were other highly qualified companies competing for valuable internet Service Provider or ISP "service fees" all across the USA. AOL and NetZero were both front-runners. NetZero's basic concept was to provide free online access to users so that after the connection was made through a singular-use modem on a dedicated phone line, an advertisement would magically appear on your screen. But, have no illusion about this period, because as the very first "pop-up" was mass distributed during this formative era, others were claiming the internet was going to be nothing more than a fad. Fifteen years later, Mark Zuckerberg would be labeled a genius for targeting pop-up ads to his customers. Nonetheless, NetZero monetized with ads only, while AOL operated on monthly fee-based revenue.

Keep in mind, as soon as digital computer technology had a chance to mingle its "dilithium crystaled" speed with Grand Canyon sized bandwidth, everything would be under the control of those who knew and understood the limitations and endured the anguish of these first online creators. Oh, how we struggled back in the 1990s.

Michael's idea, or maybe better said, the "collective idea" at

CardinalCommerce within the first few months after Chandra and Tim joined the firm, was for Cardinal to provide the same free ISP services we see above, only with a twist. The Cardinal ISP would land your personal computer to a portal, very similar to NetZero. The proposed "Cardinal ISP" would load special applications for the user behind everything visible. Now remember, net browsers were just in their infancy back then, so when you dialed in, you ended up at a place called AOL or NetZero, or some other ISP provider. It was incumbent on the ISP service provider to curate everything you saw and heard. The innovation from Cardinal was not just to provide free ISP service, but also provide the CardinalCommerce authentication application. Chandra pointed out that, with Cardinal, you were already tagged and verified for any merchant experience. What merchant wouldn't want this? The customer was pre-qualified!

Think of it this way. A limo arrives at your house with a chauffeur who escorts you to a nearby mall or similar marketplace. After each store visit the chauffeur leaves your credentials, including your credit card, encoded in a lock box at the cash register. Should you return to purchase something you are pre-approved with your personal credit limit. All you have to do is unlock the box. This is brilliant, but not exactly where Cardinal would land a year later. Because, for CardinalCommerce to do both things, provide the ISP services and provide the authentication portal, Cardinal would require a special depth of capital funding. As Michael figured out rather quickly, maybe the kind of capital that only companies similar to Microsoft could afford. Unfortunately for Michael, new troubles were looming. Here the restraints of immigration and the ironies of following the rules have huge implications for CardinalCommerce's future.

Most Americans long for an orderly immigration process. History tells us immigration has always been comparatively fundamental for improving business in the U.S. Chandra may be an excellent example here. Chandra came to the U.S. to work in Detroit, Michigan for QIS, an information technology and internet service firm, in 1997. This was a couple of years before he even met Michael Keresman. Chandra had a non-immigration HB-1 work visa from the U.S. government. It allowed him to stay here a maximum of six years, that's 2,190 days and not one day longer. Of course, these visa recipients could later apply for a "green card" if they wanted to extend their stay and eventually consider becoming a naturalized citizen. The point is Chandra was well aware of his time restriction. But that is just the beginning of his remarkable journey of coming to America.

Chandra was hired by QIS for a special ISP coding project that was to take about 12 to 16 months. And fairly significant to the story of CardinalCommerce, Tim Sherwin was lured away from STERIS by QIS at a similar time; Tim became Senior Vice President of Business Development. This was a considerable upgrade for Tim's resume and salary. Michael, of course, knew he had a dream to fulfill and always wanted to keep tabs on Tim. And so, he did. After Michael decided to get into the intellectual property business in 1999, having Tim and Chandra together was more than auspicious even though Michael was unaware he was going to hire Chandra too. Truth be told, it really wasn't difficult for Michael to lure Tim and then Chandra to Cleveland to form CardinalCommerce in 1999. It was evident, almost immediately, that the chemistry and comfort of these three men was nothing short of exceptional. Furthermore, building a technology company was a dream come true for Chandra. He wanted to see what might happen with the CardinalCommerce experiment. Chandra admitted, "I had no intention at this point to return to India to live permanently." Frankly, Chandra loved it here. After signing with Cardinal, Chandra settled in Lakewood, while Tim found Shaker Heights to be more his speed. For Chandra, Lakewood was a nifty, laid back community with an upbeat, almost hipster vibe. Life was comfortable by Lake Erie. Plus, Chandra loved being near water. Chandra had a mariner soul calling inside that he would soon live out.

These were the vibrant, crucial, and exciting days for Cardinal. Everything at Cardinal was moving pretty fast from 1999 to 2003. Chandra really thrived with this kind of energy. Plus, Cardinal was still relatively small, with only five to eight full time employees. Key personnel like Tim and Chandra maintained multiple levels of competence in varying job disciplines just to keep the company solvent. Plus, everybody inside the company knew Michael was footing the bill for all expenses for CardinalCommerce. Even now, the clear path to company marketability was still somewhat murky.

Also murky was the path forward for Chandra's immigration status.

Why? Because almost six years had passed, his HB-1 visa was due to expire and he had failed to file for "green card status" until it was too late, despite assuring Michael numerous times that he had the issue under control. Please believe me, if prior to working for Michael, Chandra was not sure he wanted to remain in the U.S., he certainly knew once he moved to Cleveland that he did not want to leave. Chandra wanted to stay. That was that.

Chandra began to explore alternatives including a "student visa" status extension. Hey, maybe the INS would accept that. Maybe it was time for Chandra to go to college! Chandra enrolled in a community college and became a full-time student.

Chandra, at this point in his life, could teach multiple computer disciplines at advanced universities like Caltech or Stanford. Enrolling at the local community college to stay a citizen is frankly brilliant. Chandra could easily ace any class he wanted, so the time commitment away from Cardinal would be next to nothing. Plus, everybody knows, student visa extensions for education are a walk in the park and done all the time. Right? Wrong!

Our would-be MIT professor, computer coding savant, ISP renegade, dark web thrill seeker came to learn that the time required to be an "actual student" for an extension is 12 to 18 months. In other words, he could not extend his visa with only a few weeks enrolled as a student. So, that was not going to work either.

In fact, in-country overstay was out of the question. This would permanently bar Chandra from ever leaving. If Chandra were to be found traveling in another country, Chandra would face a 10-year ban from returning to the USA. By now, Cardinal had global partners, so this was an unacceptable solution.

The company already had partnerships in multiple countries on three different continents. Heck, just eight months prior, Tim, Chandra, and Michael were in South Africa developing associations with two separate national banks. Ergo, Chandra would *need* to travel outside the U.S. for the company he loves. This was how Cardinal was developing, all around the world, all at once. Reality set in. It was crisis time. Chandra's H-1B visa would expire in seven days!

Enter Margaret Wong, legendary immigration attorney who handled many high-profile clients. Her customers included the brightest doctors from around the world coming to the United States most notably for the celebrated Cleveland Clinic. AMAZING! In no time, Mrs. Wong had Chandra on a video conference call with a federal judge in Washington, D.C.!

The judge in D.C. determined that Chandra's only option was to pay a small fine and then leave the United States voluntarily. If Chandra wanted any hope of coming back anytime soon, he had to leave right then. He had to leave on his own volition!

Mrs. Wong perceptively recognized how important Chandra was going to be to the future of CardinalCommerce. Now, with only three days to spare, Chandra recalled how reassuring she was at that time.

The options for Michael as owner and CEO of a new, fast growing technology business were pretty clear. On more than one occasion, one of the highly experienced board members of CardinalCommerce advised Michael to not stick his neck out too far for Chandra; that somebody else could write code for Cardinal.

Michael would have none of it. He knew instinctively what he was witnessing when Chandra first came to work for the firm. Michael saw something familiar, something that is not easily synchronized with other personality traits. Sometimes people call this a flaw that can be intellectually understood, but the emotional underpinnings are both omnipresent and suppressed. Sometimes this flaw can have long lasting psychological dominance over the individual as well. These imperfect individuals, these eccentrics, have a kindred spirit that few of us will ever experience. They are perfectly deformed. Some might say they are misfits in a way. They are cracked, torn, or scratched exactly in the same place. And only they know it when they see it. I'm afraid to say it, but most of us would have just replaced Chandra. Then again, most of us don't build award winning IP companies like CardinalCommerce.

Going forward, Michael instinctively measured the momentum Chandra brought to the team. He would not see Chandra's physical departure as a setback, but rather as an opportunity for loyalty— Michael to Chandra and Chandra's in return. Michael knew that loyalty could have exponential repercussions. He learned from his years at STERIS how powerful loyalty could be as a motivation tool, especially in battles not yet imagined. Squandering the loyalty card is a monumental mistake made by novice entrepreneurs, and one that Michael would not make.

As the deadline for Chandra's legal stay was established, destination options were discussed. His home country, India, was a non-starter due to the 12-hour time zone difference. Mexico and Canada were also ruled out due to passport requirements limited exclusively to each country after 9/11. Tim recalled that, "We needed to come up with a world class business person that can grease the skids with a 'favorable foreign government that is within a 4 to 6 hour time zone differential of Cleveland, Ohio." Did Tim just define the problem in the way that creates a solution?

It would be more than challenging to manipulate a work visa protocol for a somewhat disheveled, procrastinating Indian computer genius and move him into a mutually beneficial business relationship for a fast-growing U.S. company somewhere in a technology savvy country. Right?

All kidding aside, Tim, Chandra, and Michael were at their collective wits' end. Chandra remembered the last days, "It was crazy, non-stop, around the clock activity. We all were weary with how fast everything was moving." That was until someone remembered a little safari, a business trip and adventure to the dark continent about eight months earlier. During their business development travels, the men had met with several national banks in South Africa, as well as with Delta Singular, a payment processing company. They cultivated Delta as a technology partner, and Delta's home base was in Athens, Greece!

Stefan Johansen was the Delta Singular CEO who established a relationship with Michael back in 2001 and 2002. Once he was targeted for "The Chandra Mission," Stefan had no problem exploiting his high-ranking contacts inside Greece. Michael had made Stefan a steadfast believer in CardinalCommerce. Cardinal was the company for intelligent authentication, and Stefan really wanted to see where it was going to take business and e-commerce in the future. Frankly, Stefan was betting gold. And, just two days later (that would be day 2,186 of 2,190), Chandra was in the Greek Consulate in Chicago, Illinois being photographed, or we could say, "authenticated" for a work visa for Greece.

This is another example of a Michael business relationship concluding with ramifications for global e-commerce. Steve Mott of First Data (who we will learn about later in this book) and Stefan Johansen at Delta Singular et al., and of course Michael, molded relationships for a major payments industry merger within the next 16 months after Chandra left the country. Coincidence? It seems Michael, Tim and Chandra, or CardinalCommerce was garnering quite the reputation and influence in the payments industry, don't you think?

It is now day 2,189 of 2,190; Chandra's last official day in the USA was here. He was standing in the insufferable TSA line at the airport with a one-way airline ticket to Athens in his vest pocket. He had no idea how long he would have to stay there. Chandra recalled, "When the customs official asked me the length of my stay, I just said it was not yet determined." The only real fact that Chandra knew was that Delta Singular had a small, comfortable office waiting for him in Kifissia, a wealthy suburb outside of busy, cosmopolitan Athens. This is where Chandra would lay his head for the foreseeable future. He had no expectations. Lack of worries or living in the present is a gift granted to only a few individuals, Chandra being one.

While Chandra stood in that line ready to board a $40 million jet airplane, he did not know that while in Greece, he would help the payments industry grow exponentially. That he would frequently help Delta Singular and First Data make presentations to banks and other prospective partners. He remembered and audaciously said, "I became the *international expert* at explaining our product and platform." Chandra likes to tease.

That's right, after the airport screening as Chandra was fixing his belt around his waist, little did Chandra know, that years later he will be complementing Cardinal's international and global presence. A time when companies way less nimble than Cardinal might wish to expand in the payments industry. Also, a time when larger companies with world class assets will have a deeper respect for CardinalCommerce, believing that Cardinal's reach was that much greater.

In contrast, most companies that hire experts outside the U.S. relocate them to the U.S. for very specific reasons: to save money and to give domestic coworkers a fresh, innovative, shot in the arm. Cardinal did the opposite by sending their expert, Chandra, away. Either way, the payments industry needed people like Chandra, and Cardinal's board began to realize the wisdom Michael possessed in sticking with Chandra through the immigration saga, especially the way Michael exploited his options to the betterment of the business thereafter.

Chandra's adventure in the Mediterranean would have a transformative quality for all concerned. There Chandra would explore all the implications associated for Cardinal's mobile platform. At this time, 2002-03, the BlackBerry was the cutting-edge mobile device. It was a quality product for sure, but seriously limited in screen technology. Everybody would come to realize, in just three or four years, how "mobile" would dominate the e-commerce platform for years to come. Thinking about it now, the first real iPhone would not appear for another three years. Would Cardinal be ready?

Lucky for Cardinal, Chandra doesn't like boredom. While in Greece, he would use his spare time to map out the stratagems for writing code for mobile applications yet to be invented. Chandra's name was going to appear on no less than 40 new patents for CardinalCommerce hereafter. Solitude can be a gift, and in a place as beautiful and refreshing as Greece, what then? To answer the question—yes, Cardinal would be ready for whatever Steve Jobs would have us shove in our pockets.

Even today, to stay current, Chandra keeps a couple of code writing projects on his desk, so to speak. New technology, mobile stuff that's not going to interfere with projects already in production, are where he focuses his future ideas. However, something else would happen to Chandra. A new Chandra was going to emerge; not just mentally, socially, or spiritually, but physically as well.

Chandra recalled, "I got into running a lot. I actually was down to like 170 pounds. I was really improving myself, body and soul. Plus, my personal life was getting better and I really grew as a person." Chandra remembered a supportive group of new friends that welcomed him. "I was invited to the Island of Páros for a wedding. It was without a doubt the most beautiful place in the world." But even in this ancient Grecian paradise, Chandra would not realize how badly he would want to return to the humble small village on Lake Erie. He had no idea that, in just 11 months, he would be longing to return to his adopted home of Cleveland.

Chandra also had no idea that after 11 months in Greece, Cardinal's intellectual property would be greatly enhanced if only they could find a couple of smart technology-minded individuals to work the streets, as they say, selling the Cardinal platform in favorable European countries. Partnerships are the way to a prosperous future for financial tech businesses. And, without question, Chandra would thrive in this discipline, as his reputation was reaching legendary status. However, this was not an option for Chandra personally! After Greece, whenever that shall be, Chandra wanted to be back to the U.S. Chandra wanted to be an American!

He began the application process for his returning H-1B visa almost as soon as he arrived in Greece. Within months, he received notice of his official interview in the U.S. consulate in Athens. Chandra was not only early to this appointment, but enthusiastic to go over every single detail of his petition! This bureaucracy would scour Chandra's history binder. However, Chandra would not know this may prove to be very bad for his case. Basically, more confusing language and idioms for bureaucrats is not good for anyone wishing to reenter a country so traumatized by terrorism. However, Margaret Wong would have every word in its proper place. Chandra would be approved for re-entry into the U.S., and he would not know how much that is going to mean to him personally. Right then, he was just a guy in line, getting ready to board an international flight.

In addition, Chandra would have no idea the soul-quenching excitement the whole green card process would bring in 2008. And asking for U.S. citizenship, five years after that, how would Chandra feel about that? Chandra would not comprehend or even be able to conjure the emotions that would well up inside of him on that day in his future. Chandra can and does to this day imagine many wonderful things in that fertile mind of his, but on the day he was leaving the country, he hadn't a clue.

Chandra remembered, "You must have continuous residence in the U.S. for five years with a valid green card to apply for citizenship." Did Chandra learn his lesson? "I'm afraid not. I actually waited until the last minute, again. Old habits die hard for me. My 10 years were almost over, so I had to renew my green card for a second time. I got my citizenship in August 2018. My green card was set to expire in September a month later." Chandra raised his eyebrows, revealing that signature

twinkle of his deep brown eyes. Everything we just discussed began immediately after Chandra got on that flight to Greece.

Chandra actually remembered what he said to his best friend, Tim Sherwin, as he was getting ready to leave the country. "I told Tim not to worry because I found a really cool communication tool that worked really, really well on the internet. I told Tim that the next time we would speak with one another it was going to be on this new technology known as 'Skype.'" As he told me this story, Chandra grinned from ear to ear. How can you not love this guy?

And, just like that, Chandra boarded a beautiful Boeing 777. Moments later, he was carried high above the clouds on a jet stream to the crystal-clear waters of the Aegean and Ionian seas.

A few individuals close to the situation of CardinalCommerce asked Michael, "Would this be a sabbatical for Chandra? Or maybe just a long holiday? What exactly was going to happen to Chandra when he leaves this country? And, what exactly is going to happen to CardinalCommerce while Chandra is away?" Michael just told them, "Let's wait and see." Truthfully, Michael had no idea either.

One thing is certain: Chandra's ability to not only advance technology and communicate its intricacies, fused with Tim's informal authority inside the company and his development skills with partners outside Cardinal, secured CardinalCommerce for the future. Big companies like Visa wished they could attract employees like this.

Everyone knows extraordinary balance is a prerequisite for those athletes wishing to excel in gymnastics. And, those athletes that choose the balance beam as a discipline, well frankly they have the best balance in the world. This is exactly what Michael wished to do with his board of governors for CardinalCommerce. How to have a well-balanced board? Michael started with Ed Brandon.

An octogenarian with bright blue eyes and a keen wit, Ed Brandon claims he's 87. If my mother were still alive, she would say you can see the map of Ireland right on his face. Ed likes leaning on the steadiness of a gnarly blackthorn root, his walking stick. This one looks like it was twisted by the forces of nature, then wrenched out of the ground and fashioned into a cane by some leprechaun. I understand similar canes in Ireland are a dime a dozen. In the U.S., you will need more like $300. After just a few minutes of chatting, I realize Ed is as sharp as if he were still 37. Time and gravity have taken their measurement of what was obviously a very athletic man. Broad shoulders, big arms and hands, strong frame: That's what one sees with just an ounce of imagination. Interestingly, Ed talks softly, almost like a whisper. He clears his throat frequently which makes his voice sound a little raspy. He looks directly at his subject when conversing and smiles frequently. It's a very pleasant experience. When I'm sitting with this gentleman, I get the impression he's the kind of man that has played golf with several U.S. presidents. Only you would never know it because Ed is not braggadocios in any way. That's the kind of humility, confidence, and grace he exudes. I asked Michael why he wanted Ed Brandon on his board. This is what I learned . . .

Michael instinctively knew that to gain any respect for CardinalCommerce, both inside and outside the Cleveland marketplace, he needed to attract seasoned financial veterans from the "big three." I'm talking about banking, healthcare, and retail. On more than one occasion, these three disciplines in Cleveland have led the world with innovations, intellectual property, and life-changing patents. Believe it or not, to this day, Cleveland companies hold nearly one-third of the patents used all over the world. From basically 1850 to 1950, there were repeated ground-breaking, earth-shattering, mountain top and herculean achievements coming out of Cleveland, Ohio. However, in the last 50 years, things have slowed down a bit for Cleveland companies.

Michael set his sights on Ed Brandon very early in his quest to build a respected board. Filling board seats is an art unto itself, and Ed Brandon was exactly what the company needed. In the early 1970s,

Ed Brandon had been a loan officer for TRW Inc. Chuck Allen was the TRW CFO at the time. Allen would call up Ed and say, "I want you to loan these three guys X amount of money. Get them signed up as soon as possible. This is important, and I need it executed ASAP." That was Ed's job back then. How were they going to get the money? And, how were they going to pay for it? That didn't matter at the moment. Ed's job was to make sure that the paperwork was complete at the Cleveland branch of National City Corporation. With a wink and a nod from Chuck Allen, they would get approved. That's how business was done in those days.

Mr. Brandon went on to serve as President of the Holding Corporation and as Chairman, President, and CEO of National City. "I can remember one of my earliest jobs was to call on small to midsize companies in town. This is when I was at National City the Metropolitan Division," Ed said. "They wanted me to run around and sign up all the merchants into this credit card business, which then made no sense to me. I didn't know how that was going to make our shareholders wealthy!" He went on to say, "But gradually it became evident that credit cards would do just that." Some people forget, the credit card industry took a long time to ramp up.

Ed also recalled the very first computer that National City bought from General Electric. The chairman of National City at the time, Lou Williams, bought the darn thing not knowing that they needed to find 30,000 square feet for this massive GE computer. And the environment? The room had to be cooled to the exact temperature of 68.5 degrees Fahrenheit. As Ed put it, "All this for a goddamn adding machine?" In terms of today's dollars, that computer cost the bank $150 million. Ed continued to be a Member of Directors of the National City Corporation for an additional 10 years and retired as Chairman of National City Corporation in September of 1995.

He served on various other local boards as well, including that of Notre Dame College of Ohio, John Carroll University, The Cleveland Clinic Foundation, United Way, Cleveland Tomorrow, Playhouse Square, National Conference of Community and Justice, The Musical Arts Association, and St. Vincent Charity Hospital. Still, his all-time favorite service was his membership on the Financial Services Roundtable. With all this experience, plus a B.S. Degree in Economics from

Northwestern University and an MBA from Wharton School of Banking and Finance, it's easy to see that Mr. Brandon knew how to build community and grow commerce.

Ed came to CardinalCommerce when he was close to 65 years of age; Michael was 41 at the time. Throughout Ed's term, Michael prized the real-world experience and intellectual gifts Ed delivered to him and Cardinal.

Here is a very forward-thinking businessman that needed some guidance in entrepreneurship. Of course, I wanted to see what this young businessman could do for the emerging internet marketplace.
—Ed Brandon, 2018

However, Ed Brandon was much more than just a board member for Michael. He filled a gap in Michael's personal life too. I believe Ed became an empathetic father figure for Michael; an emotional support system if you will.

Just the same, "pleasing Ed" in business would be just as hard as pleasing any ruthless taskmaster. Why? Because all those years that Ed worked at TRW and National City Corporation had forced his businesses to be disciplined. Ed knew that important advancements in business don't happen on a whim. It's not just luck. It's not just hard work. It's not just brains. You had to be disciplined. You had to be ruthless. You had to be a slave to procedures, tasks and goals. You had to find hard working talent to advance the goals and tasks necessary to win.

Ed and the Cardinal board met monthly and discussed in great detail advancing the concept of intelligent authentication. Ed knew all along that this concept was not fully baked and that its chefs at CardinalCommerce had embarked on a true, honest experiment in entrepreneurship. If they, that is Michael and his team, could get the temperature just right, and the ingredients perfectly mixed, then maybe it would hold a nice thick layer of icing someday, not just for them, but for Cleveland too. Ed Brandon wasn't just a good advisor; he was a master baker!

When I asked Ed to comment on what Michael was like in those board meetings in the early years, Ed smiled and thought for a long time. He had watched year after year as Michael developed. Michael had to transform from CFO, to CEO overnight, which is a big difference in Ed's opinion! The word Ed used to describe Michael in the boardroom was "flexible." He remembered time and time again when Michael had this "ability to not react" to the other board members. Ed said, "Michael would keep a cool head, focusing the various talents of his directors on governing." He would go on to say, in a polite way, that the real talent Michael possessed was thinking major issues through like a chess grandmaster. Michael, according to Ed, could use overt brashness and covert manipulation with ease.

This is easily illustrated with a story about another board member, Joe Gorman, CEO of TRW. Joe relished his involvement with the cutting-edge Cardinal as they developed intellectual property for the emerging payments industry. The board execs all knew payments was going to be huge. However, Joe became critical of the timeline established by Michael for the return on investment (ROI). Let's not forget, Ed knew Gorman from his own stint at TRW. In fact, the local business community knew that Joe was an incredible powerhouse and a recognized name internationally. Michael and Ed both thought that if Cardinal was going to have far-reaching implications for commerce globally, they needed a global name on the board. Gorman of TRW was that man. His role was to facilitate gateways for international exposure, and this would require patience for Cardinal's success. In fact, it did not work out that way and Joe Gorman resigned his post, wishing to fry bigger fish another day. Joe, however, was not alone regarding ROI timeline concerns. Every day publications like The Wall Street Journal were trying to identify value for all businesses emerging in the cyber universe. It was nearly impossible back then for the average entrepreneur to grasp the fundamentals of the cyber-currency industry. Ed put it this way, "When you look how far we've come for God's sakes, in the last 50 years, it's astonishing. I have spent decades in business, and this is an extremely difficult concept to understand." Perhaps this viewpoint from Ed may have helped Joe understand the patience needed to grow the Cardinal business at that time.

In essence, these stories were fixed in Ed's mind for a reason. He knew that there was a place for Cardinal because the business community worldwide was wrestling with this problem of how to authenticate internet transactions. Ed thought to himself, if Michael could motivate and inspire Chandra Balasubramanian, Tim Sherwin, John Lazaro, Lou Schneeberger, and a powerful board of talented individuals, then just maybe he had chutzpah to not only turn a profit, but also deliver a significant return on investment.

Keep in mind, the underlying business strategy of any credit card company can be summed up as: Eliminate cash and checks. They simply hate paper money. You know cash when you see it. It's that green paper that folds into your wallet. It has beautifully etched pictures of wonderful people from history on the front side. It has numbers placed in various corners representing the denomination or value. We use it as currency to buy stuff. Yet today there is more than "green paper" currency. There are credit cards, debit cards, and retailer gift cards, and mobile phone applications that act as currency gateways by providing direct access to bank accounts.

Currency has become generational. Let me explain with this little story. I have a friend who has a wife and three daughters. The daughters are about two years apart in age. The oldest is 17. These girls are athletic, smart and very attractive, just like their mother. Plus, they are tough and competitive too, just like their father, my friend, Andy. Now, Andy is a very busy man to be certain. He runs a multi-million-dollar sales company with several employees. Andy relies heavily on his wife to sequence all the details for the family, especially during the holidays, which she wholeheartedly enjoys. Well as fate would have it, Andy was coming back from an out of town sales meeting on Christmas Eve. He stopped by the CVS pharmacy to pick up his prescriptions and found himself impulsively buying some greeting cards for all his little women. Andy scribbled in a few thoughtful words for each one. Then at the last minute, he stuffed a hundred-dollar bill into each envelope. Andy's plan was to sneak the envelopes into their stockings without anyone knowing. Adorable, right?

Well the next morning, Christmas Day, here is what Andy experienced just after he poured his fresh brewed coffee. His wife and daughters had browsed through all the trinkets found in their Christmas stockings. Andy's wife kissed him on the lips and thanked him with a squeeze on the butt. His oldest daughter gave him a hug and told him he was the best dad ever. That's when Andy looked over at his youngest daughter, Molly. She had a puzzled look on her face. Molly was holding the bill like it had cooties. With thumb and index finger pinching one of the corners, she held up the bill to study the details. Molly was in awe. Andy laughed, "Molly, it's a hundred-dollar bill." She smiled and said, "Oh, thanks dad. How much is it worth?" Andy and his wife busted up laughing! But, the reason for this this story is the reaction Andy received from his middle daughter, Kattie. Andy's middle daughter was livid with the paper currency. Kattie looked directly at her father and said, "Dad what am I supposed to do with this? If you wanted to be thoughtful you would have just gotten me a Starbucks card instead." I guess Kattie has a point. Currency has changed. It's now generational.

Kattie has a real concern. What are we going to do with our cash in the future? For years now, consumers have gravitated towards the conveniences found in plastic credit. Actually, Kattie's reaction may be more commonplace as the inconvenience of cash accelerates.

Currency, by definition, is accepted by both parties as a medium of exchange, which is an easily tradable entity to anyone else who trades with that entity, for the convenience of not using a pure barter system. Paper and coin money, cash, have been the acceptable currency since it was invented. Remember, the rareness of the currency that's being used for the transaction is only important to establish the value of the actual currency itself. In other words, if something were truly rare, the market or value would increase with demand. Let's take diamonds for example, which are not actually that rare since there are millions of trillions of diamonds on Earth. Can you imagine going to the grocery store and lining up a full grocery cart with nothing in your pocket but various sized diamonds? Of course not; that's absurd! Throughout history, currency has evolved.

Humans have altered the various accepted currencies since the beginning of civilization. Eventually, the greatest trust and agreeableness by both parties creates the popularity of that currency. The point is, a dollar bill has a "1" written on it, and a hundred-dollar bill has a "100" written on it. George Washington and Ben Franklin are only there for the ride. We assign a value, and we accept a value just like we do with diamonds. They are, in fact, only worth what someone is willing to pay for them. Here is a list of currencies that would never be used to buy a loaf of bread, a hunk of cheese, and a pile of fresh cut meats:

Companionship. Beauty. Transportation. Shelter. Knowledge or Expertise. Youth. Style. Clothing. Opinion. Imagination. Reputation. Talent. Success. Failure. Humor or Comedy. Athletic Prowess. Translation. Language or Communication. Writing. Thinking. Planning. Approval. Natural Resources, e.g. Water. Real Estate. Your race. Your sex. Your neighborhood. Your heritage. Your family name. Your tools. Competitiveness. And, of course, Intelligent Authentication.

Are these not currencies? They are constantly negotiated and valued between like customers.

You see, I have this theory that as we take cash money out of use, cash currency will become rarer. It will no longer be viewed as convertible. It will no longer be valuable. It will no longer be hoarded. That is, money will no longer be collected, reserved, and stockpiled. It will no longer feel like you have something. Let me put it another way. Have you ever lost your wallet or carelessly dropped some cash, like a 20-dollar bill? I'm not talking about stolen, that's a different feeling. No, this is on you. You were careless with your money. Has that ever happened to you? Well just consider this, if Andy's daughter lost her wallet the day after Christmas, I'm guessing she would not care about the 100-dollar bill. But, that Starbucks card, OMG she would be losing something of real value!

Frankly, digital banking doesn't feel like I have any money, either. In fact, I'm not sure my bank is even open anymore. I saw some construction where the bank used to be at the end of the strip mall. So, I drove by. There is no bank anymore. Ironically, I think they are opening a Dollar General. So, where's all my money?

My grandfather had a magnificent bank. I remember going there as a kid in the 1960s. He loved that bank. He told me he helped build it. No, he wasn't in construction, I knew that, it's just how he talked. Today, his bank is a well-known restaurant called the Marble Room. Strange, here is this magnificent building that has been out of the real estate market for almost four decades. Ornate, posh and luxurious, it must have been very costly to maintain. The volume of air to heat and cool with a room 120 feet long by 65 feet wide and 30 feet from floor to ceiling must be staggering. I suppose over time the bank holding company realized the wisdom of no longer owning and maintaining this expensive piece of real estate. They no longer needed to communicate so overtly: "This is where money is saved! And, this is where successful people come to borrow that money!" However, I find it ironic that 50 years later, this extraordinary, one of a kind, Art Deco architectural masterpiece needed a $10 million renovation/facelift to become a newly viable commercial restaurant operation. Oh, it's exquisite today. I was in awe in the 1960s when I was there as a child, and I was in awe a few weeks ago, when I was there for a distinctive dinner celebration. Come to think of it, when the waiter handed me our bill, I thought, my grandfather probably made his deposits here every week. Only his weekly deposit from one of his trucking companies back in the 1940s was probably less than the cost of one appetizer today.

I would like to conclude that it was Ed Brandon's last comment that may actually keep me up at night. I asked Ed, where were we headed as a society with currencies being conveyed online? Ed looked at me and confessed that he has no idea. Mr. Brandon explained that the modern view of money is difficult for him to comprehend. He said, "What worries me now is the safekeeping of all the world's currencies because the electronic network can abandon ship at any time." Well Ed, "In God We Trust."

Takeaways:

1. Be disciplined, ruthless and a slave to procedures, tasks and goals
2. Build respect for your company by attracting front-runners
3. Do not react—be flexible—but stay on your timeline
4. Find your Best Man—treat him well
5. Enhance your "informal authority" leadership skills
6. Assessing employees is a full-time job
7. Loyalty!!!
8. No worries—be in the present

Scene 3: "Take a Message"

Kerry had been around. Even with a few gaps in her resume, she really wanted to settle into a place she could call home. Kerry can be very convincing with just enough charm. In her interview she really wanted to do phones. She said so many times, "she loves phones." Cardinal at the time had grown to over 60 employees. The influx of inconsequential phone traffic was driving all the techies crazy. Dropping everything to answer silly questions was slowing up production and operations. Everyone wanted Kerry to work out! However, Kerry's messages were poorly written and illegible almost all the time. Plus, Kerry's attitude after week three started to slip. It even could be felt on the other end of the phone line. She was mostly gloomy, commented one employee. Now the whole company had a problem with Kerry. Only no one wanted to tell Michael. Not to worry, another week and it will be fine. Nope, Kerry was even worse. The flood gates opened, and the complaints poured into Michael's private voicemail. What was Michael going to do? Certainly, an underling can manage this issue. Not a chance! Michael began to study the dilemma. A week later he had the solution.

Michael's first move: a promotion for Kerry! Once he is charged with a task, the likelihood of him letting someone else take over is nil. Michael explained that her new promotion meant some new responsibilities. Because after all, the phones don't ring every minute, therefore she could do other valuable jobs to "stay busy." So, that day Michael personally worked with her. Michael sat next to her, discussing her job description and responsibilities. Michael explained, once she mastered these new little jobs, more remuneration was in order. When I say Michael worked with her, I mean that he never left her side. He stayed with her every single minute. He was super positive and encouraged her to death.

At first, Kerry thought, "I can play this game too. This guy is the President CEO of a big company. He has to get back to more important matters than working the phones." Well, she was wrong. Michael had been underestimated most of his life, and this was just one more way to prove it. Not for himself! This task was visible for all the new employees at Cardinal. Michael wasn't interested in sympathy. He was demonstrating his attention to detail. He was showing everyone how much he cared about his company. He showed them that he listened to their needs, even for something that may seem small and insignificant.

Well, one day turned into two on Michael's mission for excellence. Snickers at the water cooler were subtle, and maybe even undetectable. He said nothing to anyone, and this was critical. He pretended like he didn't know when this was going to end. Michael offered nothing but encouragement every step of the way. Michael taught her to be very careful while signing her initials on every phone message. They worked on penmanship and key phrases repeated often by callers. Michael went on to say that her initials are the authority of doing your job with excellence. Her initials are a sign to the world that you love your job. Michael went on to teach her a few basic office filing techniques, too. He even demonstrated how to set up mailings. He shared the importance of every little detail. Well, two days turned into three and then four. "If Cardinal is going to be successful, it's because everybody must pull their own weight," Michael would relentlessly repeat to her.

Michael watched closely; he knew his student was getting a little bothered with all this attention. Michael instinctively understood the bigger issue at hand. Simply stated, Kerry had never been held accountable. Plus, Kerry was sometimes aggressive and two- faced to other employees. Michael instinctively understood every company gets someone exactly like Kerry every so often. These people could slide through any system.

That's when Michael dropped the bomb. Michael was watching and waiting so patiently, sizing up his competition, after all, Kerry represented the impediment that keeps the company from winning. Then, when Kerry least expected it, Michael was going to lay out something so revealing, something no one had ever said to her in her whole life.

Michael was going to tell her the truth. Michael stated, "As long as you work at Cardinal, I am going to stay right by your side. I really want to see you succeed."

Well, it was more than she could handle. There was no day five. It was Friday and Kerry called in sick. The following Monday Michael learned that Kerry had quit. Michael must have made an impression on Kerry, as she wouldn't even come back to pick up her last paycheck. Michael had it delivered in an overnight envelope that required her initials.

CHAPTER 4

Think Tank Tinkerers
& Tokenization

Intelligent Authentication—
Encrypting a Fistful of Dollars

People ask Michael all the time, when did he know for certain that CardinalCommerce was going to be a significant player in e-commerce? Mr. Keresman usually smiles and says something like, "Er, right after every board meeting," or he might say, "When CardinalCommerce, 'The David' defeated Visa, 'The Philistine Giant', in an intellectual property battle." This took place in 2004, in Australia of all places. Some have speculated that Australia was chosen as the battlefield by Visa because should Goliath not win, it would be less conspicuous to customers.

However, a few industry insiders were expecting a game-changing technology from Cardinal well before the first Visa lawsuit. Some say they knew when Michael crystallized his business objective into one key phrase. In the early days, Mr. Keresman likened Cardinal's IP as the "encrypting a fistful of dollars." Basically, this means that when you are logged in with CardinalCommerce, you're already authenticated and approved to purchase just about anything your heart desires, and this is from the convenience and privacy of your home!

Michael always perceived the Internet as being similar to the Wild West of the early 1800s. In so many words the Internet gold rush had overwhelmed all the lawmen available. The badlands were full of bandits and thieves lurking. Honestly, e-Commerce was terrifying at the turn of the last century. That's when our sharpshooting entrepreneur, Michael rustled-up his posse, CardinalCommerce. Michael just knew a bounty could be had should he be successful in bring safety, security and trust to the marketplace.

Years later in 2012, Tim become a total believer when he observed, "Oh, my God, this crazy payment industry that WE created is actually going to become all that WE imagined!" And here is why Tim had this observation.

Cardinal had learned everything there is to know about the industry standard, Three Domain Secure, better known as 3D Secure. Visa commissioned Arcot to build integration authentication payment software for issuers and merchants years ago. Here we find a business strategy by Visa that ultimately benefited Cardinal. Visa accommodated the larger merchants, such as Target, Walmart and others with their authentication screening software. Visa's strategy: With nowhere else to go, smaller merchants would just fall in line thereafter. Michael realized a more effective outcome was possible. "Let's extract the complexities away from the merchants and away from the banks." Michael asked the merchants to evaluate a critical question; "Can you build and maintain intelligence screening in house, or should you move that burden to someone else like Cardinal?" The answer is so obvious today. Merchants don't have the time or money to be so encumbered with authenticating a buyer. They need to deliver customer service to real consumers, not screen fraudsters, or evaluate if buyers can't pay.

Visa had ordained 3D Secure to run the transaction among a cardholder, merchant, and banks. Perhaps it was an attempt for Visa to help underwrite the bank's liability. In essence, Visa told the banks, "Don't worry about it. We will take care of the fraud." However, only the most sophisticated merchant could afford this liability. In fact, it was the thousands and thousands of smaller merchants that won the day for CardinalCommerce.

Think about it for just a second. Cardinal, a tiny off-the-radar company in nowhere Mentor, Ohio, a suburb of Cleveland, basically spent a dozen years creating software for the internet payments industry. Cardinal had learned everything there is to know about 3D Secure and all the other integration payments software. And frankly, 3D Secure had a negative reputation with most users across the industry. Plus, the entire network had the potential of saying, "We are tired of this! No more 3D Secure! We are going to try something else." Cardinal could be holding a ton of infrastructure with nowhere to deploy it. Michael was always conscious of this fact! He was always trying to find other ways to validate their technology. He never stopped believing in their capabilities. While everyone else may have worried, Michael never stopped thinking: We are making something unique; we are creating something wonderful. We are building it the way it is supposed to be! Again, 3D Secure had a negative reputation with most users across the industry because it slowed up the checkout process and resulted in lower conversion rates. Consumers abandoned transactions because of confusion and long buffering time. Tim likes to call this part of the transaction "the chaos."

In the early days, when a merchant tried to authenticate a transaction, it would go out to the cardholder and sometimes not connect. Users would be left with a blank white page due to a variety of issues, including issues with the merchant's website and the customer's browser or device. This was a horrible user experience for consumers. It would tarnish the merchant's own brand name. After a few bad experiences, consumers would not want to return. They would try to find the product somewhere else. Frankly, it may not have been any more user-friendly than before. However, the point remains; the customer went elsewhere. Merchants were frustrated with the process because Cardinal's software was supposed to enhance sales and shift liability and fraud, but sometimes in the blink of an eye the sale was gone altogether. Tim reflected, "That was always the big rub, why we couldn't get massive amounts of adoption."

This became the greatest of all hurdles for Cardinal. Michael went back to his old playbook; Michael believes the solution will always be found in how you define the problem in the first place. Once the problem is properly defined, the solution is clear. Michael pushed his key technology developer Chandra to simplify the problem.

Michael fully understood. "Because no merchant or bank will allow any access inside and behind their firewalls, Cardinal will need to extract the transaction away from their systems." Once Cardinal had the transaction inside Cardinal's software, Michael knew success for Cardinal was imminent. That meant Chandra knew he had to build a design specification to not burden the merchants with software plugins. That's it! Cardinal's software lifted the burden away.

Here is how it breaks down. Cardinal claimed they needed more data from the user: browser, issuing bank, location, card, buying habits, etc. So, in response to 3D Secure, Cardinal developed the Centinel software. Just like the word sentinel as "guarding and protecting," Cardinal's Centinel software guarded and protected the transaction inviolate. This is the platform that would interface with the merchant's software to complete the integration of the sale.

When a customer went to click "buy," Cardinal's software now redirected the transaction to a Cardinal window, where it would be subject to Cardinal's scrutiny. Now, Cardinal was in control. Cardinal would run the analytics on the transaction. Once it identified 70 or 80 different data points about demographics, buying habits, frequency, location etc., Cardinal could tell the merchant with assurance when the customer goes to Bank XYZ on a certain web browser—Netscape Navigator, MacWeb, IBrowse, Agora or whatever—the transaction returns 95% of the time in two seconds. However, when the customer goes to Bank LMN on a mobile browser—java script, ajax, or whatever—-they return 43% of the time in four seconds. Cardinal's Centinel eventually would collect 160 or more data points about the customer and the transaction. If data points did not properly align, Cardinal could lower the assurance of the legitimacy of the transaction. This was the foundation of what made Cardinal really take off. They even gave it a name: Rules-based Authentication. Centinel enabled the Rules-based Authentication and all the millions of little things Cardinal does behind the scenes that complete the transaction for the issuing bank, the merchant bank and the customer.

Cardinal didn't want intelligent authentication to slow up transactions or hurt the conversion rate. Michael believed from the beginning that Cardinal would aspire to do the opposite. Rules-based Authentication gave merchants the ability to set their own transaction restrictions and rules. YOU, the merchant, can decide if the transaction is approved based on a predetermined threshold. "Hey, merchant, when you use Cardinal intelligent authentication software, we will tell you: with this bank, and that browser, on this device, or on that device, this is going to be your conversion rate." That was the breakthrough for the company; merchants were no longer subject to the friction and "chaos" from different banks. For example, a young 23-year-old, living in Los Angeles, is probably moving around more frequently than say a 40-year-old in Dallas. So, there is less weighting on the home address for the individual in LA. Therefore, based on other known data, there may be more weight placed on spending history, vendor name and location, frequency, buying habits, etc. Extrapolating this example, let's say LA on one occasion wants to buy triple the normal amount at a competing drug store, not the store he or she normally uses. This would raise a red flag for all concerned. The home address of the user would be less important. Mr. Keresman reminds us, "Even though we were collecting valuable data, Cardinal always remained loyal to the merchants' and banks' wishes." Cardinal never sold any data to outsider, third-party suitors. What merchant would want Cardinal to run credit cards if they were selling information about their clients? The benefit of using Cardinal's authentication was now as clear as can be: The merchant had less fraud, more sales, and paid less per transaction.

Cardinal started gaining visibility. Tim said that by this time, "The buzz was really growing for Cardinal!" Cardinal could demonstrate exactly what was going to happen to every cardholder across every bank, across every device. The comfort this gave Cardinal's merchants and banks was immeasurable. They went from "the chaos" and a frenzied environment to one of total control. Plus, even in the worst-case scenario of the issuer's system being down, which frankly happened all the time, Cardinal was still in control of the browser session. Cardinal could hold everybody together in Cardinal's system. Often Cardinal could pull them back into the transaction, if the problem was severe enough.

To this day Michael credits Chandra for Cardinal's breakthrough moment. However, Chandra does not agree one bit. Chandra insists that Michael deserves the credit for setting up Cardinal for this remarkable turn of events.

The Cardinal Sales Department

How Michael built the sales department and strategies at Cardinal can only be classified as distinctive. Traditionally in business, sales are the lifeblood of the company's future. However, there was nothing to sell in the early years. It was all research and development. So even from the beginning, sales at Cardinal were not relegated to a department or division. Michael always stressed that for Cardinal to be successful, the whole business was to be one huge sales force. He made sure everyone at Cardinal was selling the concept of CardinalCommerce. But let's step back for a second.

Let's look at what was really going on in 2000 through 2003. The more you talk to the employees of Cardinal, the more you realize that it is not a traditional company. Cardinal was simultaneously educating an industry, building a brand, and developing IP. The sales group and Michael's vision for the future of the payments industry were, in fact, the same thing. Michael was so good at this that his investors never stopped investing. One board member and investor stated, "What started out as a small innocuous investment for me turned into a multigenerational family trust venture."

Even today, Cardinal's "sales department" operates nontraditionally. Functions that get institutionalized tend to be hard to shake, especially when many or most of the players are legacy kinds of folks. If this were any other operation or organization, sales would be driving the campaigns for its future success. At Cardinal, the salespeople have always been semi-autonomous. As one former employee states, "Who doesn't like being semi-autonomous? Who doesn't like doing what you do the way you want to do it, when you want to do it?"

So how did this come to pass? Let's look at fraud. PIN debit had become the prominent method to eliminate fraud in the early face-to-face commerce days. In the store, the purchaser would just sign the receipt or enter in a PIN depending on whether it was a credit or debit transaction. But in e-commerce, the user couldn't enter a PIN instead of signing. Today, this method by definition has been excluded from e-commerce because all of the rules and regulations around security don't work in e-commerce. The basic tenant of PIN debit is to never give anyone (including an online merchant) your PIN number. The encryption that is required by a PIN debit method must follow a set of rules, and this is contrary to the rules Cardinal uses in e-commerce. As a payments executive pointed out, PIN debit was excluded from participating in the fastest growing segment of the payment space because its fundamental security strength, not sharing a cardholder's PIN, would be compromised in online retail. All the things they built to be more secure than signature-based products, like Visa and Mastercard, were incompatible with the way that internet commerce evolved. By 2005, there were 10 or 12 payments processing companies in the U.S. But after the recession hit, as things got tighter, they started to dwindle. Perceptive observers have pointed out that the real reason the payments industry launched slowly was because no entity existed to bring various stakeholders together to consider internet security. There were merchant groups. There were issuer groups. There were Visa and Mastercard, of course, who were principally driven by self-interest. None of these, at that time, had online security as a high priority.

Paul Turgeon, before he became a consultant for CardinalCommerce, recognized this variation facing internet security protocols and decided to do something about it. Several highly connected individuals formed a think tank under Paul's urging. This sole purpose of this new entity, the Secure Remote Payment Council, was to create a middle ground for banks, cardholders, and merchants. Paul added people like Mimi Hart, the president of MagTek, Inc., a POS terminal company, Ron Congemi, former president of the STAR network, Dennis Lynch, the former president of the NYCE debit network, and Pete Hart, the former president of Mastercard. They met on the phone once or twice a week to build their mission. Security in e-commerce, principally for debit cards rather than credit cards, became their new focus. Eventually, Michael learned about this group. He knew that this was going to be a unique opportunity, and this was all based on one fundamental belief: If Cardinal was ever going to be recognized for its true potential, it must be first noticed by the status quo.

We can clearly see the truth in Michael's statement, as Secure Remote Payment Council's fundamental mission today is less directed purely at e-commerce and more focused on giving entities other than Visa and Mastercard a chance to survive. The council, a not-for-profit organization, runs entirely on donations from its board seats.

(For more information on Secure Remote Payment Council go to www.secureremotepaymentcounci.camp8.org.)

CardinalCommerce was an extension to Mastercard and Visa's 3-D Secure. Cardinal's two product suites were inside what was known as the Universal Merchant Platform. Centinel (for merchants) was one and 2-IDentify (for issuing banks) was the second. Insiders observed that they may have been obscure in the early days, but clearly started to gain significant traction in 2008. Michael knew all along that a market for this technology would eventually emerge. Maximizing Cardinal's IP would be his end game. It wasn't like there were many places where Cardinal's IP instantly fit. There still aren't. This can be understood from the perspective that we really don't live in a centralized society. There are very few amalgamated things even today. Look at it this way. You have your Social Security Number, which makes you part of the U.S. population. With that and only with that, can the government impose a certain standard. Or, look at your driver's license and the standards imposed on your behaviors through that centralized or federated structure.

Therefore, if CardinalCommerce, an unconnected company in Mentor, Ohio, was trying to be relevant by promoting an idea to an industry, what would it be? If Visa and Mastercard had *not* funded 3-D Secure, what would Cardinal have picked to promote? There was undoubtedly no other opportunity. Experts believed the only place Cardinal could have thrived was through 3-D Secure. Ultimately, Michael was proven correct. Visa basically said, we also have to own it, meaning Cardinal's platform. Look at PayPal. It couldn't have possibly survived without Visa and Mastercard, either.

This little company with a handful of employees and a bunch of pending patents found a place to apply all it had. Essentially, enabling authentication (validating the identity of cardholders) between cardholders and their issuing bank could provide assurance to merchants that the transaction was fraud-free.

Cardinal was more defined by what it was *not*, rather than by what it was. True entrepreneurs like Michael often spend more time clarifying what they are not! Cardinal was not a consulting company. Cardinal was not a software installation company.

In reality, Cardinal was one of the first "cloud" based companies that banks, merchants, and consumers could use to ensure transactions were safe, secure, and without fraud.

Cardinal's cloud-based platforms distilled the complexity out of the vast internet so that these respective parties could communicate with each other at the speed of light. Imagine the complexity of a system that involves billions of consumers, millions of merchants and tens of thousands of banks located worldwide. Then add exponential components such as multiple devices (laptop, tablets, mobile phones, etc.) that use different multi-version software, communication protocols, and security measures.

What Cardinal did was create two platforms that could understand any communication protocol: The Universal Merchant Platform and its sister platform 2-IDentify for banks. In addition, these platforms recognize the device, then translate, encode, and encrypt and route transactions from any place in the world to the desired destination.

If Michael did not have the money, and did not have the belief in himself, he could not have spent seven years without revenues. Many insiders believed that merchants hated 3-D Secure. Many insiders claimed that banks found it very cumbersome, too. We know Visa and Mastercard were not going to support it. Then how in the world did Cardinal become necessary? Perhaps a little story about another Cleveland entrepreneur may fit here. It's about a guy named Rockefeller. He developed an industry, just like Michael. He built a brand, just like Michael. He cornered the status quo with his intellectual property, just like Michael. He developed the product and the process at the same time, just like Michael.

The parallel here is simple. Gasoline was a byproduct of the distillation process of making kerosene. This was the poor man's illuminant in the late 1800s. It was highly desirable because kerosene was relatively stable to use, mostly odorless, and burned for a long time. It was also cheap to make. Rockefeller and other kerosene distillers around Cleveland were making kerosene as fast as they could. Demand far outweighed supply. However, they had no use for the distillation byproduct, gasoline. Gasoline was highly volatile, smelled awful, and could not be controlled. In fact, it most often wound up illegally dumped in the rivers and lake around Cleveland. Because gasoline is less dense and floats on top of water, it was ignited and burned on some occasions. The waste product, gasoline, that was hated and repudiated by so many, became one of the most important inventions the world has ever known because of its potential. It is this same attitude of "how should it work" that Michael fostered in CardinalCommerce and that can be found in other thrill-seeking entrepreneurs. Lest we forget the status quo, Visa and Mastercard did not want to eliminate every competitor. If Visa or Mastercard tried to do a controlled burn like what was done on Lake Erie in the late 1800s they would be caught in their own flames. Cardinal was just as volatile as gasoline because of Michael.

"If you are not this type of competitive person, you should rethink being an entrepreneur." —Michael Keresman 2018

If you look at it one way, the marketplace is unaffected by Cardinal. The company fit a niche. It was an early adopter. By being an early adopter, it got market share. This gave Cardinal visibility which Michael defended like a bulldog.

The idea of centralized architecture, that Cardinal was so instrumental in bringing along and exploiting, would have its day with Visa as a dream or a nightmare. And we will soon find out.

Card Not Present—CNP

The growing concern, unfortunately, was that there is no "signed" receipt outside of face-to-face commerce. Visa and Mastercard initially compromised their operating rules to allow merchants' CNP transactions with one major caveat: the merchants must accept the entire risk of fraud liability when there is not a signed receipt. As such, the acquirer and its merchants had no recourse but to absorb 100% liability for fraudulent transactions. This added significantly to the processing costs for the merchant, who then paid higher fees due to the inherent risk and the loss to the cost of sale. They would also receive chargeback fines in the range of $25-50 per transaction and the potential loss of the customer for future transactions. On average, the potential cost of

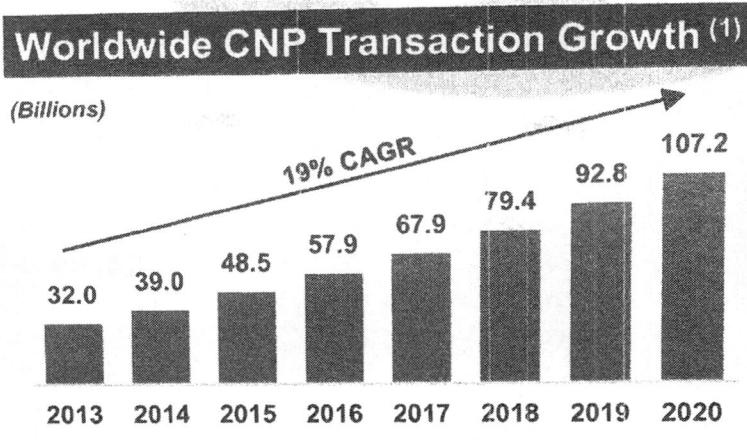

internet transactions increased by $5 per transaction in the "card not present" world.

To control the costs forced upon merchants and their acquiring banks, many additional intermediaries and processes were added to mitigate some of the risk. However, these processes did not protect the merchants and their acquirers in the event that the transaction was charged back. These systems merely aided the decisions as to whether a transaction should be accepted based on risk factor. Often, these measures had unintended consequences. Some of the transactions, known as false-positives, were actually made by loyal, honest, and payment-worthy consumers. In other words, the good guy, based on risk analytics, was deemed to be a crook.

Every internet-based transaction required more intermediaries than a card-present transaction as a result of the additional systems, processes, and personnel required. Thus, internet transactions cost considerably more to complete. In essence, the increased cost was the responsibility of the merchants who had failed to protect themselves from the liability of fraud and chargebacks. In addition, merchants risked turning away valid customer transactions because of false-positives, which often included any transaction from a foreign country.

The aggregated risk of fraud as a percent of attempted revenue transactions is between 4.6% and 7.8% for physical products, and between

14.4% and 23.5% for digital products. The range varies depending on how stringent a merchant is on accepting orders that have been validated via address verification services, says an industry periodical, CyberSource. The value for the acquirers and their merchants can be found as all "'card-not present" transactions would face a 100% liability for disputed fraudulent or unauthorized transactions due to a lack of a signature.

In January 2000, the Wharton School of Business uncovered that, per capita online, retail spending declined from 1998 to 1999. Were the best days behind us? Many inside the business community were using words like "fad" to describe online e-commerce. Wharton's conclusion for this downturn in business was that it resulted from credit card security and privacy concerns. Ernst & Young also weighed in on consumer concerns regarding internet transactions, stating that credit card security was the primary barrier to acceptance of e-commerce.

The expected convenience, as well as the lower prices associated with internet commerce, were the positives. However, future growth was offset by consumer concerns regarding fraud and ease of use. Mainstream media also was not on the side of e-commerce, as major stories of stolen account numbers and pilfered customer information flooded the news cycle daily.

Annapolis, a premier credit card consulting and research firm, estimated cyber-fraud between 1% to 20% of all online transactions in 2000. At that time, electronic merchants were under increased pressure from Mastercard and Visa to find solutions for eliminating fraud. Failure of these merchants to reduce fraud levels resulted in fines of up to $100,000 per month and potential loss of merchant status.

Merchants' reactions to these pressures were two-fold: First, they employed preventive merchant systems, and second, the merchant attempted to camouflage the level of fraudulent transactions. WHAT? Camouflage the fraudulent transactions with more fraud? But that's not all. Brand erosion and the perceived negative value of the company by consumers was on the rise!

Merchants, financial institutions, consumers, and the credit card companies have always been vulnerable to brand erosion when consumers become encumbered. We know that hackers have been successful many times in attacking merchant servers. In a few cases, hundreds of thousands of credit card numbers were actually published on the web, as was the case with CD Universe, an online music retailer, back in 1998.

Additionally, an MSNBC story reported that the network obtained a letter, sent by Visa to member banks, to inform them that a hacker stole 485,000 credit card numbers from an online merchant, and then stored the massive database on a U.S. government web server. The letter was forwarded to MSNBC from an anonymous employee of the Navy Federal Credit Union to highlight the fact that some financial institutions were tragically inadequate in protecting consumers.

Let's jump to 2005. I would like to demonstrate how an aggressive brick and mortar retail merchant, Forever 21, adapted quite well to its sassy, young, tech-savvy female consumers. Back then, clients or consumers would purchase an item online and then have it "shipped to store!" The merchant offered a decent discount to the consumer. Estimates were that nearly 65% of the online shoppers purchased additional items once in the store, boosting growth both through the internet and in-store.

However, fraud had taken an interesting turn here, as verification steps at the store were often not well policed by the point of sale staff. In-store pick-up fraud remained one of the largest loss items for major retailers. Maybe not for Forever 21, but certainly for many others, especially electronics. For example, consumers could now go online with a stolen card, buy thousands of dollars of fancy, electronic equipment, show up at the store with a fraudulent ID, and walk out with merchandise that had already been paid for.

Faced with costly back end cost-detection fraud systems, the net effect was that internet merchants paid for fraud five times: 1. lost sales due to the lack of consumer acceptance, 2. cost for fraud prevention programs, 3. penalties imposed by the credit card, 4. actual fraud losses and the related charge-backs, and 5. the actual loss of the item stolen— or cost of goods.

Depending on merchant size, the total cost in 2000-2005 ranged from 4-12% over the purchased price when including: discount fees, transaction fees, fraud screening, fraud penalties transaction adjudication, and additional personal requirements related to processing a transaction. For some merchants, costs were so enormous that it prevented them from even accepting credit/debit cards. Moreover, these high costs even forced some merchants out of business.

Who in their right mind could afford to start an e-commerce business? As a result, the overall average cost to process a transaction as estimated by Michael was an increase of at least 4% compared to that in face-to-face sales.

As a result, merchants then gravitated to Address Verification System (AVS), which became the most common process used to authenticate buyers in a non-face-to-face transaction. The idea was simple: by comparing the billing address to the address-on-record with the consumer's issuing bank, merchants believed a resolution to fraud was imminent. However, within a short period of time, the numbers proved otherwise as AVS only provided a marginal impact on fraud reduction. Plus, legitimate consumers were declined for various reasons such as change of residence, or when the "bill-to" address was international. Stop-gap solutions, such as AVS and other fraud-reduction software, fraud-screening telephone or e-mail verification, resulted in no shift of fraud liability either. In the long run, fraudsters quickly learned and adapted new techniques to circumvent hurdles placed by merchants. Meanwhile, merchants continued to absorb fraud losses and margins were ultimately squeezed throughout the fraud-screening services world.

Michael realized another important obstacle for e-commerce was the ease by which consumers made it from shopping basket to checkout. Studies showed that nearly 30% of new consumers abandoned the transaction once they decided that verification requirements were too time consuming, cumbersome and/or personal.

With the enormous potential for the internet to evolve into a major marketplace, merchants were desperate, and Michael knew it. "Consumer acceptance" was, and still is, the buzzword for e-commerce. The creation of a perceived safe, secure, and user-friendly e-commerce environment could change the world forever. Michael understood the major obstacle to gaining mass-consumer acceptance of e-commerce was the lack of user authentication. If the preservation of privacy could also be achieved, other inherent shortcomings of the credit/debit processing systems would be marginalized. Michael had no place to turn. Credible studies on the matter were yet to be created.

The solution for CardinalCommerce was clear. e-commerce must be simple to use, easily understood, portable, and relatively transparent to be accepted by consumers. Transparency, along with friction free checkout, were key.

So, beyond consumers' fears and beyond merchants' liabilities, Michael made a bet on himself and his team each and every week. The merchants must eventually be freed from the traditional liabilities associated with fraud because they do not control these credit/debit payment vehicles in a non-face-to-face world. That was one huge conclusion to make in the year 2000!

Michael focused on security first. If no credit card number was used, there was no credit card number to steal. A single-use sixteen-digit transaction number prevented any unauthorized or duplicate charges. A two-factor authentication positively identified that the proper account holder was accessing the account.

Privacy was the next objective: no name was released; no credit card information was released. The consumer controlled the release of any personal information to selected merchants. Plus, anonymous shipping capabilities were present.

One industry colleague, Steve Mott, remembered when he first heard about Michael's concept of "tokenization." He recalled the brilliance of CardinalCommerce's tokenization patent and the number of times he had to remind his superiors at First Data of how innovative of a company CardinalCommerce was developing into at the time. Steve was building a career anticipating the magnitude of digital technology. He knew payments was going to be big. And, he liked Michael Keresman's ideas.

Tokenization was Michael's new technique for security. Although it was conceived in 2000, it would take an additional 10 years before the rest of the business world even began to ponder the true potential of online e-commerce.

> Why would some guy with such a comprehensive resume of financial systems for the health and medical equipment industry know something about tokenization? But obviously, it occurred to him.
> —Steve Mott 2018

Steve goes deeper, "So, there's a difference between an idiot savant, like Jay Walker at Priceline, and Michael Keresman. Jay could come up with a hundred crazy ideas, really brilliant ideas, but only two of them were winners, and the other 98 were a waste of time. Mike, on the other hand, was very parsimonious with his ideas. One of those ideas that deals with security is based on a brilliant and simple concept. 'Compromising or hacking a system is really hard if you don't know what it is.'"

Here is what Steve is saying. If you look at a work of art, you just might say, "That looks like a work of art." Now, this painting that you are looking at may actually be an authentic work of art or it may be just something that looks similar to an original work. Either way, you are looking at some paint arranged on a canvas and you are trying to evaluate or compare it to something else from your memory. Well, this painting may look like a Matisse, or something else like a portrait from my favorite impressionist, John Singer Sargent. No matter what pops into your mind, you kind of know what you are seeing.

Now imagine taking all the paint—the exact amount in all colors— off the canvas and rearranging the paint somewhere else. Imagine this with a really famous work of art, maybe one very complex and beautiful like Vincent Van Gogh's "The Starry Night." Everybody knows this painting; it has long been considered by the art community as one of the greatest pieces of art of all time! However, the paint is now rearranged in a completely different way. Don't be confused here. You are looking at the same number of brush strokes and quantity of paint in thicknesses and in colors. It's all exactly the same, but the brush strokes are completely positioned in a new way, perhaps vertically arranged or stacked. Or maybe the canvas dimensions have changed (the original "The Starry Night" dimensions are 2'5" by 3', an area of 1,044 inches).

So, as you are looking at this crazy painting, someone from the art world, a real highbrow critic, says to you, "Oh I'm sorry, I can see you are confused. You don't have any idea of what you are looking at, do you?" This frumpy nitpicking art critic, in his dark rim glasses and moth-eaten suit, is so dour you wonder if he has a pulse. He goes on to explain his brilliant observation, "This is *The Starry Night* by Vinn-nn'cennnntt, . . . Von Gok." Of course, you laugh to yourself and think— this guy is an idiot. Everybody knows you pronounce the artists name "Vincent Van Gough."

Well, that's "tokenization" by CardinalCommerce.

Let's take a credit card. A plastic card with all this information, that can be compromised a zillion different ways, is both amazing and obtuse. Virtually anyone can use a credit card, which explains why credit card debt has been climbing for decades. Steve Mott elaborated that a big chunk of CardinalCommerce in the early years was built on this very simple premise. "Michael looked at the credit card and thought, 'Well, why don't we just disguise it and make it a token?'"

Steve also pointed out that for years nobody cared about what Cardinal was doing, "The big guys like Visa and Mastercard thought, 'Why change the status quo?' In fact, the industry was beleaguered by its penchant to preserve the status quo pretty much since the beginning. And really for one reason, the interchange." The interchange is the fees the card companies charge for their service.

Consequently, if the interchange were reduced, which, of course, all merchants would enjoy, or if we could reduce the hidden costs of using cards in the first place, we could really make a big impact for all concerned. As we know, a portion of the cost of using a card is to pay for fraud. It's a huge cost to the system.

One thing is certain, we would have a healthier marketplace if we could reduce all the hackers and data breachers. Just consider how many lawsuits originate due to fraud! Of course, it's the interchange that is affected by Cardinal's ability to eliminate false-positives.

Look back to the early 1990s to see how we all got to this moment for CardinalCommerce. Steve Mott worked on a program called SET, Secure Electronic Transactions Protocol. It was simply an attempt to wire credit cards securely on the internet. The "networks" are bank card networks with a four-party model. There's the cardholder, the issuing bank, the merchant with an acquiring bank (better known as a merchant bank), and the network itself holds everything together. This whole arrangement constitutes "a payment."

Imagine if all parties involved in a payment conversation could see each other without anybody else peering in—then we would have a secure payment. Steve's solution to accomplish this was to go through a certificate, a digital certificate, which is kind of like a token. Everybody would have an individual certificate. Microsoft, IBM, Netscape, and a whole bunch of other companies like RSA (a computer network security company with a focus on encryption) understood that Cardinal would be able to take the certificates and say, "This certificate is valid. It's never been compromised," so they could make a payment online. Doing it this way was a new concept. But not entirely, as RSA had tried a certificate idea on its own. RSA's idea was no longer current with the latest technology. When Steve did the very first transaction that was supposed to model SET for the future, it was at the White House in 1998. Steve was working for Mastercard at that time. Steve likes to point out that Al Gore is a huge nerd for technology, and he personally witnessed the first transaction. IBM, a partner with Mastercard, was there too. When a credit card was presented for a purchase in those days, there were two basic techniques for gathering the information for the transaction: a "knuckle-buster" (set the card on a small hand device with the receipt over top and slide the bar to squish the numbers onto the receipt) or a "mag-strip" transaction. Mag-strip gathered the information electronically from the tape on the back of the card. Both techniques took between 5 to 10 seconds for the process to finalize. But with the new SET system, as the digital certificates were exchanged back and forth, the process could take 30 to 40 seconds. Doesn't seem like much, does it? This created customer friction because it added time to the checkout process. Who wants to stand around a POS terminal or wait for website confirmation for 38 seconds? The drawback to this "security" was time and complexity. Note that these examples place the credit card and the owner of the card together at the time of the transaction. Card-Not-Present or CNP transactions were a different animal all together.

RSA was running the protocol, and Visa and Mastercard were slow to realize that this process was premature. Michael's tokenization of the individual card was just two or three years away, and it was a lot easier because the card information never left the customer!

Now, I'm not even sure Michael knew what he had at the time. Tokenization, nearly 20 years later, is still disruptive to some. It's still expensive, and not everyone trusts it. But it did help establish an early brand for online payments, and one of the initial customers of CardinalCommerce was PayPal.

Consumers buying over the internet became even more impatient

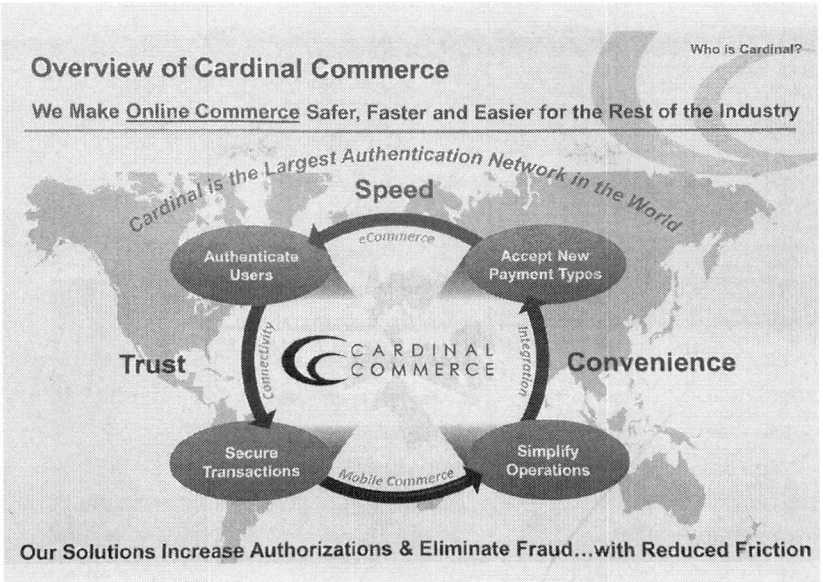

and did not want to wait for an email confirmation. CardinalCommerce came up with the PayPal solution. Here is how it works. Stick another digit on the front of the 16-digit scan. That's the token. PayPal sends that to CardinalCommerce. Cardinal strips off that one little digit and submits the transaction on your behalf, in real time, to get the authorization. It then goes back to PayPal. Then, PayPal says, "You're good to go! That was a good transaction." In fact, Cardinal was doing a considerable number of PayPal's transactions.

The lesson here is easy to understand. When Michael looks at a problem, he becomes a business model engineer. He tinkers, like most engineers do, but he comes up with something that's very basic. Michael challenges himself, and he challenges the people around him with, "Is this going to work or not?" Drilling down on a binary outcome of "going to work or not going to work" is really hard, but the "maybe" is gone!

Steve Mott said that when First Data initially looked at CardinalCommerce as they were considering businesses acquisitions in the payments industry, First Data said Cardinal's solutions were too simple. They needed to be more complicated. Steve recalled how a few of the top executives at First Data disparaged Michael to no end, "Who's this nut running CardinalCommerce and why does he think he can solve these big problems that others have been pondering for years?"

Beginning in April 2003, any merchant using Cardinal's software was no longer liable for a disputed transaction regardless of authentication by the issuing bank. The merchant would still receive payment for a disputed transaction. This created an enormous value proposition to the merchant/acquirer. Furthermore, in some global regions, Visa and Mastercard implemented massive price breaks for merchants/acquirers who were enabled by this process.

By 2005, Cardinal, Arcot, and a couple of other minor players became the arms and legs for Visa and Mastercard to tumble their way forward with "Three Domain Secure." Michael was tinkering away for other clients trying to solve other problems. His mantra remained, "There must be a simple way to do this. Is this going to work or is it not?" This was Michael's binary code, once again.

Keep in mind, had Congress not passed the Electronic Signature Act with President Clinton's signature (ironic I know) on June 30, 2000, none of this would have mattered. Michael's journey with his fledgling company was destined by a major force never experienced in commerce.

Michael would champion the possible solutions. He would chat it up with clients and knowledgeable industry captains. This is what provoked First Data and Visa the most. The status quo, Visa, Mastercard, and First Data, etc., granted permission and handed down systems and techniques. The status quo never admits not knowing. Hubris is a way of life for the status quo. Steve remembered thinking; Mike was not a troublemaker. He's a problem solver. He may be eccentric in his problem-solving path. And we may not understand how he communicates. But we need to take notice.

Many times, I would just go out to Cleveland to see Mike. I liked to discover what he was doing, because Mike was always tinkering on concepts and productive solutions nobody else would even consider.
—Steve Mott, 2018

Steve noted, "If you don't look like them maybe you are not them." He said the two things that brought Visa to the table in the end: 1.) Michael sticking it out for as long as he did, and 2.) *NOT* being from Silicon Valley.

Near 2010, CardinalCommerce became financially independent. That's a decade of unrelenting belief. Now Cardinal was profitable with reliable and verifiable market share. Michael would never hold his success in contempt to the credit card conglomerates by saying, "See, I told you." Michael got his satisfaction by solving problems. These big companies were way better funded and with much lower risk factors. Steve recalled asking, "Mike, how in the hell can you put up with these guys?" Steve was referring to Mastercard and Visa. Michael would chuckle with no real answer. However, Steve believed it was Cleveland and the Midwest attitude that gave CardinalCommerce its charm for success. Steve said, "Cardinal is not threatening. It's just a bunch of honest people, working for an honest wage. Basically, they were working on problems that other people didn't want to do or couldn't do." There were 10, 20, or even 30 companies in Silicon Valley that thought they were too special or too important to collaborate with Cardinal. However, when we look at the payments industry today, 90% of Cardinal's success came about because of tinkering.

Steve Mott and Michael Keresman were way more than just old timers prospecting for gold on the internet. At the very end, I imagined these cowboys on their horses riding towards the sunset. Actually, truth be told, the last time Mike and Steve were together was in their usual spot at the country club, sitting in Adirondack chairs, smoking and drinking in the twilight. Either way, it was easy for me to feel the warmth and glow of their long careers together. Remember, Steve was a non-employee, a think-tank tinkerer from 2001 up to the time of sale. Over all those years Steve and Michael got to know each other very well. Michael thought so highly of the relationship he offered Steve some stock options in his rising company as far back as 2001. But for whatever reason, Steve never formally presented Michael with the paperwork. Steve admits now that he lost the paperwork sometime later. Well, right before the financial transaction for the sale of Cardinal was almost inked, Michael asked Steve to forward his options to the company. Of course, legal counsel was involved, making sure there were no improprieties. Steve said, "Typical of Mike to find ways to go above and beyond humanity. You'll never find that anywhere else but in a place like Cleveland, Ohio."

Cardinal Accidentally Builds
Venmo and Launches PayPal

Today mobile banking has become a multibillion-dollar business. However, while Cardinal was tinkering with various applications to manage 3D Secure, they stumbled into a process that changed everything. Today, everyone has heard something about mobile banking, mobile alerting, and mobile payments. However, back in 2007, Cardinal was building an application that allowed the user to connect two separate bank accounts with complete security. This capability was through SMS, or Short Messaging Service. In essence, one user could send 50 bucks from his or her bank account to another bank account with no friction or cumbersome verification episodes. Today we know this to be Venmo. The only drawback then and now is that the user could make an error with a decimal point resulting in a catastrophic judgment on his or her bank account. There is no resource for modification once the transaction takes place. However, the takeaway is that Michael created an environment and shepherded along ideas that resulted in companies that are now household names. We know them as PayPal and Venmo. Now that is tinkering on a grand scale.

Takeaways:

1. Validate your strengths daily
2. True entrepreneurs ask, how is this supposed to be?
3. Frenzied chaos can lead to innovation
4. Associate with tinkerers
5. Clarify what your company is NOT
6. Your industry, your IP, and your brand is exactly who you are
7. If you don't look like them maybe you are not like them
8. No need to spike the ball in their face, the game is not over just yet

Scene 4: "The Brass"

For the most part, fudging timecards, or the padding of one's arrival and departure on site, was the preferred technique for spurious wealth creation in the construction industry. An extra hour or two each week could add up pretty quickly, especially for skilled union labor and when overtime was calculated in as well. Quality owners and management in the construction industry knew well that controlling labor costs could be a give-and-take scenario under the best of circumstances. This was why Michael was hired right out of college. He was to add sophistication to the job site, and that is precisely what he did. However, after he put a sharp pencil on payroll, he turned his attention elsewhere. He started with the "keys" to all the locks found on the job site. Little did Michael know "security" would become a theme that he would exploit for the rest of his life.

In a multi-shift construction operation, everything must be locked up and then reopened by the next foreman when that shift began. That's when the "brass" became important. The "brass" was a 3x1 inch piece of metal made out of brass. On one end was a ring of keys and on the other was a hook so that it could hang up easily in the job supervisor's trailer. In the event that an employee needed a key for a piece of machinery or a supply trunk, it would be on that shift manager's brass. So, each brass had a corresponding employee number embossed in the brass. Now, why would you emboss an employee number on a piece of brass? So that it couldn't be changed easily.

Well as the story goes, a young Michael A. Keresman, fresh out of college, noticed extra keys would often be tossed into a large Maxwell House coffee can that sat in the job trailer. Michael pointed out, "Did you ever notice, people really don't like to throw away keys?" Well, when a key went missing from someone's brass (often intentionally lost to cause job delays), invariably a copy could be found in this Maxwell House coffee can. Michael noticed when this occurred, all the workers would stand idle, sometimes for long periods, as the foreman searched for the replacement key. The coffee can would be turned upside down and spread all over the job site conference table. That's when Michael stepped into action. He asked the job site superintendent if he could have a go at solving this annoying key conundrum. "Well that's why you are hired, to help with inefficiencies found on the site," was the response from his boss.

First, Michael applied the time honored and tested system of a color-coded ledger. Red was the master key; it stayed home. Orange was upper field management. Yellow was for foremen, etc. Your brass had the keys you needed to keep your crews working efficiently. When you showed up for work, you got your "brass." Then Michael applied the next level of security. Additional locks were purchased, and a rotation of locks was employed. Gas tanks, hand power equipment, large tools, small tools, and all kinds of supply lockers were involved. Everything of value had a lock. I bet you can guess what happened next. The job site "black market" was coming to an end.

Unfortunately, when a nefarious someone would get a hold of a manager's brass, duplicate keys were made clandestinely. Of course, pilfering would then ensue. However, with Michael's new system the result was nothing less than astounding! Gas tanks lasted 15% to 20% longer than in previous weeks. High use tools and power equipment lasted months longer. In the end, the boilermakers could not be blamed for steeling the carpenter's equipment or vice versa, because the keys would never cross over!

Michael remembered that early on, long before anyone had figured out what was really happening, a "tough guy" came into the trailer. "Hey, Sam sent me in to pick up his brass. Would you get me Sam's brass?" Now let's remember, Michael is not a small man, but he recalled looking up to this monster of a man. Michael's response, "No, I'm not going to do that. Sam needs to pick up his own brass." Well, apparently this guy got a little hot under the collar. Michael remembered once the confrontation turned ugly, he told the guy, "Well you can probably kick my ass, but you're not going to get those keys. And then, I'm going to have aggravated assault and battery charges brought against you." Michael then took a small breath, "Now would you please do me a favor, and tell 'Sam' he needs to pick up his own brass for himself." As it turned out, "Sam" never showed up in the trailer because he wasn't even on site that day, and the tough guy wasn't even under Sam's jurisdiction anyway.

CHAPTER 5

Intellectual Gamble
& The Outback

All the world is made of faith, and trust, and pixie dust.
—J.M. Barrie, "Peter Pan"

Let's see if the government might lend a hand in this inelegant authentication business. Michael's strategy in battling the status quo involved every aspect of the economy, including banks. However, here he would find a certain weakness. Most banks had these really old "legacy systems" that were put into place years and years ago by the government to help with regulations. Michael likes to call it, "government overreach."

Typical of the U.S. government, if they don't understand how a business is creating commerce, they find a way to regulate it. Then once they do understand, they create a way to tax it.
—Michael Keresman, 2018

Since the beginning of the computer age, banks were controlling large volumes of raw data. However, creative or innovative correlations were hard to make. At the time, from the 1970s to the early 1980s, banks clearly had the best computer engineers, and the government knew it. The banks could afford it! The government was constantly adding regulations to keep the banking industry in check. Ultimately, the "legacy-bag systems" that were established for the banking industry had to be converted to work over the internet. This may not have been the most complicated technology problem, but it became an important business problem and an important distinction for CardinalCommerce. Why?

> Banks are not known for rapid change. They are the epitome of the status quo. Cardinal had to first adapt to them. Then, Cardinal would find a way to grow together with them.
> —Michael Keresman, 2018

What Michael learned while implementing this process was simply amazing. Basically, one element inside a bank wasn't regulated directly. However, because so much of the rest of the business was regulated, banks operated like the whole business was regulated. This was the opportunity he was looking for. Now Cardinal had a chance at putting its software ahead of everybody else. Plus, Michael knew banks abhor variation. Adjustments cost money. Adjustments slow down decisions. Change hurts business, because the status quo owns the formula for success. All the related barriers to entry have been vetted, scrutinized, and secured so that everything stays the same. When everything stays the same, they win. So, Michael took the old IBM machines that were still working in the banks and put an interface into one of their quirky little systems. Then, Cardinal connected the front end and pushed all the transactions through Cardinal's authentication capabilities. In the end, Cardinal didn't solve the hardest technical problems; they went and solved the real business problem that was hard to solve.

Did Michael luck out? The very fact that the status quo would allow old technology and machines to be used and reused again, and again, created the opportunity for Cardinal to control its own future. If you want to understand how to challenge the keepers of the status quo, you must first understand what they have earned on their own. Once you know what they know, once you understand how they earned it on their own, then over time you can modify what they have. The greatest opportunity comes when they ask you to share your insights. Not to overthrow the status quo, but to re-establish yourself inside the firmament that they created.

Michael's not a revolutionary. His methods are not revolutionary. His technology is not revolutionary. Michael believes he is evolutionary. There's a huge difference here, and it's the reason why Cardinal was sold for such an amazing price in the end.

Cardinal's centralized systems were able to extract the complexity of "computers talking to each other" by taking a message in any format or language and then translating, encoding, and routing that message "from anyplace to the right place, in the right way." This eliminated the cumbersome and error fraught status quo approach in trying to create common languages, codes, and processes between multiple systems, multiple devices, multiple protocols, and all the communication networks in the world. Cardinal's business then became, how do we get all the banks to sign on? One bank by itself isn't enough.

Michael asks, how many software "Silicon Valley" pitches begin with so called entrepreneurs saying, "As soon as we get to a million customers, we're going to make all kinds of money?" What Mr. Keresman said was, "Forget how you are going to get to the millionth customer." Mr. Keresman went on to ask, "I want to know how you are going to get your very first customer? Then we can discuss your plans on getting to the second, the third, the 10th, and so on."

Michael understood that volume would sustain the revenue for any bank's business model. But really, he just focused on just "one" bank first.

> How do I get from zero to 10 or from zero to 100, or even to 10,000? Whatever that number is, how do I get from zero and still be around to influence an outcome?
> —Michael Keresman, 2008

What I want to know, how do you keep a workforce in place and focused for a 10-year overnight success? Well, one way that Michael kept Cardinal from floundering was with the loaded labor rate. If Cardinal could keep its loaded labor rate low, and then retain and reward its talent, Cardinal had a fighting chance.

So yes, Cleveland was a factor in Cardinal's success! Cleveland has a competitive "loaded labor rate." This gives nearly all start-ups in Northeast Ohio a significant advantage over the rest of the country, if you can find the right talent!

The loaded labor rate is defined as the additional costs, such as taxes, benefits, etc. which increase the actual employment costs to hire an employee. It is sometimes referred to as, "the fully-burdened labor cost," which is the full hourly cost to employ a worker for the hours he or she actually works, which includes wages and the "burden" of the additional costs.

The Midwest May Have Lower Salaries, But Buying Power Is Higher Similar to CardinalCommerce how average computer programmer salaries with the cost of living differ between San Francisco and other Midwestern cities					
			Percentage Cheaper Than SF		
City	Salary (avg.)	Adjusted	Housing	Utilities	Groceries
San Francisco, CA	124,000	-	-	-	-
Cleveland, OH	76,000	143,000	-76%	-9%	-11%
Madison, WI	94,000	170,000	-70%	-8%	-18%
Chicago, IL	90,000	140,000	-57%	-21%	-14%
Minneapolis, MN	88,000	165,000	-71%	-21%	-15%
Columbus, OH	84,000	120,000	-79%	-32%	-21%
Detroit, MI	84,000	169,000	-74%	-11%	-28%
Indianapolis, IN	84,000	177,000	-78%	-15%	-26%
Omaha, NE	84,000	177,000	-75%	-25%	-25%
MIDWEST	85,500	182,700	-73%	-18%	-20%

Adjusted = Equivalent salary in San Francisco, based on buying power
Data via C2ER Cost of Living Index (Jan. 2018)   Zachary Crocket, The Hustle

For Michael, finding talent for his team was more like watching a bunch of college kids play beach volleyball; Michael could spot the real good players in two minutes. Basically, not enough can be said about sifting talent for your company. Some entrepreneurs just have the knack for attracting innovative, creative, and hard-working employees. As the graph demonstrates, Silicon Valley tech programmers have been known to make anywhere from 50% to 150% more salary. However, on average, Michael knew he had a competitive advantage. CardinalCommerce could hire 2½ engineers for every engineer in Silicon Valley.

As Michael likes to point out, most of the tech engineering efforts at Cardinal were incredibly complicated.

Michael once asked a Silicon Valley CEO, a very self-aggrandizing industry czar bred exclusively from the West Coast:

> Wait a minute, how are the Silicon Valley engineers so different from their colleagues in Cleveland? Are the Cleveland engineers not solving the exact same kinds of problems?
> —Michael Keresman, 2008

Tim Sherwin remembered, "Once Chandra was focused on an engineering technical problem, everything else on his desk became unimportant." Chandra would never stop until he solved the problem. It was not unusual for Chandra to focus on an engineering solution for 60%, 80%, or even 90% of his time. Relentless, goal-oriented employees like this are so rare.

In hindsight, CardinalCommerce may have been way ahead of the curve with internet e-commerce, but there were similar companies expanding at the same time. As an example, Numerical Technologies, a nifty innovative software company, was developing in Japan. Numerical Technologies focused on financial risk management and consulting. They specialized in high performance computing (HPC), parallel Monte Carlo simulation, and financial modeling.

Founded in 1998, Numerical Technologies became a leading software company aiding the top-tier banks and insurance firms by licensing technology and patents to focus on the semi-conductor industry and the iPhone. Both companies, CardinalCommerce and Numerical Technologies, faced identical issues with the status quo of the banks from their respective countries. Both companies found a way to grow with the banks through partnering and solving problems simultaneously. As a side note, in October 2010, Numerical Technologies established an office in Singapore to advance its software development and R&D capabilities and to pursue growth opportunities outside Japan. Today, estimates range between 70% to 90% of the iPhones used are fabricated with technology established by Numerical Technologies.

However, all this technology involved embodies a quarter-million patents. For every such patent in technology, there are hundreds of other technologies that are all included. Exponentially speaking, millions of technologies meld together to make one iPhone work.

But just like Numerical Tech, Michael and his team needed to find their own way in the world when all these other tinkering engineers and startup companies were offering complimentary technologies.

The First Lawsuit

Michael understood from the very beginning, from when he was just a boy, that a major component of being successful was being able to stand one's ground. He knew Cardinal could protect its IP. He knew this would have a lasting effect on Cardinal's success. Frankly, he was just waiting for the moment to happen. However, just because Michael can defend his IP once, that doesn't guarantee Cardinal can survive all the intellectual property wars that are sure to follow. Even though the market started to recognize that Cardinal had valuable intellectual property, that didn't stop highly visible and world-famous organizations from trying to take down CardinalCommerce.

Cardinal's first IP battle was with Visa . . . in a world far, far away. An unfertile desert, as it is sometimes called. Visa chose to do battle in Australia!

The nuances of international patent law would be cumbersome for Cardinal. For instance, patent applicants in Australia must post publicly their stated invention for a period of six months before the patent office could even issue any approval. More or less, the patent office in Australia was stating, "We will grant your patent if no one opposes you inside the six-month posting period." Visa opposed Cardinal's intellectual property and patent on the last day of the six-month posting period. The last day! What was Cardinal to do? This was Visa; they could afford all the king's horses and all the king's men to find any evidence, no matter how sketchy, to exterminate the pesky little insect, Cardinal. Visa could intimidate any insurrection in any territory with a blink of an eye. Perhaps other companies similar in size and expertise to Cardinal would have thrown in the towel, but not Michael. In a unique counter-effort, Cardinal sent its U.S. patent attorneys, the ones most familiar with Cardinal's technologies and inventions, to Australia. Their mission was to "help the local council." Frankly, the Australian patent council was afraid of the payment giant Visa, too. Think of it. Cardinal had two months of expenses and attorneys in Australia. Would it be worth it in the end? You bet! Actually, the Australian patent office appreciated Cardinal's legal team thoroughly. They had no problem granting Cardinal its patents and ruling against Visa's claims.

One blogger famously reported, "Cardinal is credited for a 'giant win' against Visa." It should be noted in Australia it is customary for the *challenger* on a patent case, Visa, to pay court costs and legal fees. The blogger later added some wit to his post by saying, "Visa will just put all the legal fees on their credit card."

Cardinal, the David, had beat the Philistine giant, Visa, to the ground. The world would never be the same. Cardinal gained not just recognition for its software, but also international recognition of its patents, inventions, and the inventors themselves. The way to derail Cardinal's IP wasn't on the international stage. In fact, under the direction of Michael, Cardinal previously applied for a European Business Method Patent in the European Patent Office, which was virtually unheard of for any company outside the European Union. An American company with a European Business Method Patent, no way!

> Then he took his staff in his hand, chose five smooth stones from the stream, put them in the pouch of his shepherd's bag and, with his sling in his hand, approached the Philistine.
> —1 Samuel 17:40

Cardinal's board members had their first big sigh of relief. It was clear that their investment and related risks were more than defendable.

The Second Lawsuit

Just because international patent offices began to recognize Cardinal and its inventions didn't mean that all rivals would simply capitulate. In fact, here in the United States, a well-financed third party attacked Cardinal by giving away a look-alike technology for free. A reprehensible CEO of a small technology firm in the South brazenly made public claims against Cardinal. Scandalously he stated, "Why would you pay

Cardinal when you can get it for free from us?"

Patent lawsuits are complex, time consuming, and very expensive. Any one of these could hypothetically knock Cardinal from its perch. In this particular case, Cardinal was way out on a limb. The pretender's strategy was to cause market confusion while engaging Cardinal in a lengthy trial and lawsuit. Its weapons were the resources of time and money. It was sponsored with almost unlimited financial means. Its owner was the richest man in Mississippi. This man had thousands of employees and 20 or 30 different companies from various sectors of the economy. However, he had only one small technology-oriented company. Interestingly, the owner was unaware of the shenanigans of his technology CEO, despite the CEO's overt arrogance. This CEO established in the marketplace that "his experts" were ready to testify that Cardinal was not the original inventor of its IP. Plus, the rival firm already made a broad sweeping challenge at the patent office, too. It claimed in writing at the patent office that absolute proof would be disclosed that Cardinal was the true fraudster here! Michael was incensed. "Actually, no matter what you say about this man, the attaching firm's CEO and his narcissistic tendencies, Cardinal really couldn't afford more confusion in the marketplace over our IP." Michael went on to say, "Cardinal was making significant strides at the time." Many technology insiders detected that a lengthy trial similar to the one in Australia could dismantle Cardinal's future success or worse, ruin the marketplace for everyone.

Michael calculated his vulnerability again and again. Cardinal was legally 10 steps behind in every way. In fact, the rival filed an illegitimate suit against Cardinal in the courts, too. Michael realized a trial in Mississippi needed to be challenged, adding more time. Trial in Ohio would be better but challenged by the rival—which would again add more time. This was a dark time for Cardinal. Confidence was very low. Michael insisted that no Cardinal employee was to talk about this lawsuit in any way.

However, there was one glimmer of hope. The Cardinal legal team learned that patents can be challenged at the patent office, or they may be challenged in the courts. But not both! That's when Michael realized that Cardinal needed to use the exact leverage the challengers established from the beginning of their assault. Michael did the unthinkable. He agreed to a trial in Delaware! Simply put, Cardinal outmaneuvered the predator by petitioning the court for an early trial date. The big-headed CEO and his public statements were used against his conniving ways. Cardinal's attorney persuaded the judge that these previous statements at the patent office by the rival CEO indicated he and his team were prepared for a trial. Cardinal's attorneys co-opted this because of the rule of dual challenges mentioned above. Cardinal would relish a quick trial. In fact, the rival CEO had made so many numerous public statements that the courts MUST grant a timely date. In essence, Michael knew that because his attorneys were already experienced in defending this technology in other patent battles, there was no time like the present. In the end, because of the accelerated timeline by the presiding judge, the predator CEO and his company withdrew their claims and left the marketplace forever. Amazing! Just like that it was all over.

Eventually, the wealthy owner of the technology firm in Mississippi was brought up to speed regarding his nefarious CEO. Frankly, the wealthiest man in Mississippi was infuriated that his reputation had been tarnished by such a reprehensible man. So, let the record show, upon realizing that one of his employees made illegal and slanderous attacks about CardinalCommerce, the wealthiest man in Mississippi made a public and in-person apology to every single Cardinal employee. The man flew his entire technology team to Cleveland to do so!

Well, in typical Michael fashion, the whole event turned into a festive party and celebration with all concerned, minus one CEO. Michael beamed with pride for CardinalCommerce.

So, what happens next for CardinalCommerce? Let's see, now all Michael needed to do was fly across the galaxy, grab R2D2 and the hidden plans stored in his memory, fly back completely undetected by the evil empire and Darth Vader (who can sense everything), then exploit the knowledge and fundamental weaknesses in the Death Star and save the day. Simple, right?

For CardinalCommerce, plugging Michael's "R2 Unit" into the Death Star's mainframe, which in this metaphor is the banks and their legacy systems, was nothing short of fantastic. It was like plugging into every business that wanted to sell online. Getting a piece of each and every credit card transaction could be worth billions, or so Michael thought.

Michael believed that, eventually, all online credit card transactions would have to go through some filter or cleanser. If you ruminate on what Michael and his crew were trying to accomplish, you will quickly realize this is actually a very long and very laborious mental process. Maybe the whole world, or parts of the world, doesn't trust or want to be put through the CardinalCommerce filter system.

The Richardson Way

Monetization can come in thimbles, cups or pints. But it just might show up in buckets!
—Michael Keresman, 2018

According to Michael, monetization for Cardinal would come three ways, but in only three ways: 1. market share, 2. innovation, and 3. personnel. Many believe the ultimate valuation of a business is determined by market share; or is it? Would Cardinal be innovative enough? Would Cardinal have enough of the market share? Would Cardinal's talent stack up to the rest of the world's? It was so important to Michael that Cardinal had to be top tier in all three metrics. There was no question after the multiple rounds of funding and hectic growth that took place, Cardinal needed a little polish. Michael took control of the message being delivered to the rest of the world.

How could Michael take control of his message for the next phase of the monetization process? How should people be talking about the creation of technology owned by CardinalCommerce? Hubris aside, Michael once again went outside his company and his expertise and found patent attorney Kent Richardson.

Kent remembered that from 2012 forward, Cardinal was focusing on numerous business strategies simultaneously. As he put it, "Cardinal needed stronger internal focus." The most important area to target: the message encompassing the portfolio of patents. How to talk about that portfolio was not easy, and here is why.

Michael and the team were upping their marketing game pretty much every quarter. Kent basically said, let's just be a slave to the website for a short time. Let's make sure all of our customers and all of our competition get the same message. Let's put together a strategy and re-position the portfolio when talking to people from the industry, our customers, and even the general public. Let's tell the Cardinal sales team exactly what to say. Then, and only then, can we get the continuity in the marketplace. Because in the patent industry, if somebody asks a pointed question about your product and you don't answer it correctly, you can find yourself in a lawsuit.

Michael realized everything was in that one message delivered by the employees of Cardinal. How to talk about that portfolio became his new obsession.

As Kent pointed out, the industry really isn't concerned one bit about what you have. Cardinal's patents, who cares? Kent says it's just like a gun in your back pocket. He remembered talking to the Cardinal sales team, "Now, if I tell you about the gun in my back pocket, you just might treat me differently. So, if you tell people you have patents, they are going to think about the fact that you have patents. And if you don't tell them, and frankly a lot of people don't, you're going to get no credit for having them. This means the first thing you have to do is tell them. The reason you want to tell people is because you don't want to *surprise* them."

Kent says many lawsuits today are caused by surprising a business about the "illegal" use of a patent!

> One of the worst things that can happen inside your company is a representative discovers and accuses another company, "Hey you are using all of our patents and you need to stop now."
> —Kent Richardson, 2018

The truth is, most people simply don't know they have infringed on someone's property. A constant heard in most patent battles is, "How was I supposed to know?"

Of course, a company should know. They should have done some work and researched first, but many don't. Frankly, with the speed at

which companies grow, most are accustomed to the concept that no one looks anymore. If you're not going to acknowledge that industry people don't look, then you're going to surprise people and piss them off. At that point, they end up countersuing you.

At Cardinal, Kent worked closely with the Marketing VP, Tara Lavelle, to help reposition the way the patents were marketed. They established a timeline on the website. Cardinal's historical timeline of technological innovation and business successes became the very center of its web presence. The patents were all there for all to see.

The road map of how Cardinal created its incredible intellectual property and how it was solving critical business and technical problems was no longer debatable. It could not be debated in any court. Cardinal could then say, "What do you mean you're surprised? It's all been on our website for X number of years!" Now, Cardinal had taken away the moral outrage of being surprised, which is what starts litigation.

> Because, ultimately, if you are given a 20-dollar bill or a credit card, you're trusting that it's not fake. You want to believe in that currency!
> —Kent Richardson, 2018

Mr. Richardson has booked nearly $700 million in patent licensing in his 30-year career. Think of it this way: Cardinal's currency is its own currency. Intelligent Authentication is as human as you are. No one can vouch for you like you.

Takeaways:

1. Stand Your Ground—a smooth river stone between the eyes will do just fine
2. The Status Quo hates change—work together, be clever
3. This is not a revolution, this is an evolution
4. You can dream about millions of customers; let's just get one customer first
5. Narcissists, and billionaires: learn to deal with them
6. Market share, innovation, personnel is how you will be remembered
7. Always cultivate expert advice outside your comfort level and company

Scene 5: "Code name"

Not enough can be said regarding Michael's voracious appetite for professionalism. Michael insisted his employees advance competently on a schedule. He required the manifestation of true excellence especially when it counted most, which Michael calculated in advance. One of his goals for Cardinal was the finest assembly of professionals possible. However, there is a lighthearted side to Michael, too! This is evident with Michael's insatiable curiosity about everyone and everything that revolves around him. It simply never ends. Usually, Michael will learn just about everything he needs to know about someone while they are completely unaware. Michael does this by engaging in little games or diversions. Some might call them competitions, while others might say they are more similar to a practical joke in nature. Either way, Michael creates frivolous, playful, upbeat and silly events all day long. His employees think he's just being funny. Actually, Michael is collecting data. This is the data he will deploy to prompt his staff to a higher level of achievement when he needs it most. Michael does this, all the time.

One of Michael's little amusements in business can be seen in a game of inclusion and exclusion. He started this game that later evolved into a clever managerial technique so many years ago while guiding STERIS. Michael would create funny little names for projects and assignments, code names if you will. Then he would decide who exactly was going to be in on this little secret. If you were not needed for a project, you were simply not included, and that's that. However, this did not place anyone beneath anyone else in the company. Why? Because virtually everyone had a named project on Michael's menu. Therefore, everyone at Cardinal was important. Everyone had a project at one time or another with a code name. Here is the kind of conversation Michael might have with an employee in the hallway or lunchroom that demonstrates the power of this managerial technique. "Hi Mike. Hey just to let you know, I'm finishing up 'Cold Stone' today. And then Chandra needs me to look at 'Operation Dodge and Parry.'" At which time Michael might respond by saying, "When Henry signs off on Cold Stone, then Dodge and Parry . . . OK?" Wait, what? What just happened? Could the transfer of information be any more efficient?

Michael made up a distinctive code name for every company-wide project, too. A clear understanding of the objectives, strategies and tactics to be deployed were reckoned into his label or code name. Very often, Michael would get into the minutia defining the exactness of what the project entailed. However, the true magic was in the name! Not just any name but one uniquely fit for each project. From the onset Michael would introduce the code name and the participants. Michael's theory: The name tied the project to an easier method for remembering the specifics, the activities and duties associated within. I must say, if I were a visitor at CardinalCommerce and I witnessed the interaction we see here with the owner of the business; I would genuinely want to be an employee of CardinalCommerce. What a fun culture to create while at work.

Here are a few examples.

OPERATION CODE NAME: ANACONDA

LEVEL OF SECURITY: Top Secret

MISSION DETAILS: Find the personnel inside American Sterilizer (AMSCO) responsible for the pending FDA penalty. Demonstrate superior management controls at STERIS to guide and then kindly push the FDA to lift the penalties for a favorable timeline for redeployment of IP holdings. If need be . . . quarantine rogue parties responsible. Ultimate focus—garner a majority of shareholder proxies for an all-inclusive takeover of AMSCO. Demonstrating FDA approval of STERIS for redeployment of assets is KEY. Essentially swallow whole a company five times STERIS' size.

MISSION LEADER: Bill Sanford

FINANACIAL ARCHITECT: Michael Keresman

MERCENARY SPECIALISTS: McDonald and Company

TIMELINE: Six months and that's it!

SIGNIFICANCE: Imperative—This is the future of the sterilizer industry!

Why Anaconda? This code name chosen by Michael indicates the opportunity the FDA created by paralyzing AMSCO for its alleged falsification of technical information. The FDA placed various penalties against AMSCO for an extended period of time for these IP violations. Essentially, upper management at AMSCO had lost control as erroneous assertions were made by lower managers and technicians regarding the AMSCO IP and product. STERIS was uniquely positioned to swallow a much larger company that was paralyzed or smothered in the penalty period. Of course, a real anaconda functions this way in the wild.

OPERATION CODE NAME: OTTO GRAHAM

LEVEL OF SECURITY: Top Secret

MISSION DETAILS: Not only defend CardinalCommerce IP from fraudulent claims made by Mississippi technology company, but help secure the marketplace for future operations overall. Reposition Cardinal's reputation by isolating false declarations made by scallywag CEO. Pull the Cardinal team together to defend, compete and win.

MISSION LEADER: Michael Keresman

MERCENARY SPECIALISTS: Patent Attorneys

TIMELINE: Immediate

SIGNIFICANCE: Imperative—this is the future of Intelligent Authentication!

Why Otto Graham? The Cleveland Browns played football in the All-America Football Conference, or AAFC, just after WWII. This league was considered junior to the NFL. Simply no one believed any team from the AAFC could compete against the mighty teams in the NFL. The Browns emerged with a berth to play in the NFL in 1950 after the AAFC folded. The Cleveland Browns were labeled by the press as outliers and underdogs. History will show the Browns went on to appear in the next six NFL championships, winning three with Otto Graham as the quarterback and team leader.

Obviously, Michael loves football and saw himself as the quarter-back of a team that was labeled the underdogs. There is no question in my mind that the industry was expecting Cardinal to fail when challenged at this new high level. Interestingly, even though Cardinal had just beaten Visa in Australia, morale at Cardinal was low. The press and industry insiders discounted Cardinal's achievements, claiming its victory was inconsequential and a fluke. Michael used Otto Graham as inspiration for himself and his team at CardinalCommerce to take on their next challenge.

OPERATION CODE NAME: TYCHE
(PRONOUNCED "TI-KEE")

LEVEL OF SECURITY: Need to Know, Only

MISSION DETAILS: Present CardinalCommerce to co-opt a self-reliant strategic partner for a total affirmation of intellectual property created, current workforce established, and market share earned with a favorable sale of CardinalCommerce.

MISSION LEADER: Michael Keresman

SPECIALISTS: Chandra and Tim

TIMELINE: Immediate

SIGNIFICANCE: Imperative—This is why we worked so hard!

The name was so obscure that no one inside the company would figure out what was happening until Michael was ready to reveal its meaning. Tyche was the classical Greek mythological goddess who guided a Greek city to good fortune and prosperity. She appears frequently on ancient coins and in architecture. Michael once said, "How could there be a more fitting name for the process which led Cardinal to its ultimate destiny, the sale to Visa?"

OPERATION CODE NAME: DODGE AND PARRY

LEVEL OF SECURITY: Top Secret

MISSION DETAILS: Confuse hackers and cyber attackers with never-ending alternatives.

MISSION LEADER: Michael Keresman

SPECIALISTS: Chandra

TIMELINE: Immediate

SIGNIFICANCE: Imperative—Reputation is on the line!

Fairly early on, Cardinal was a prime target of hackers and those seeking ransom. Typically, nefarious organizations would threaten to flood a company's website with so much bogus traffic that, in effect, the business would have to shut down. Unfortunately, if a company capitulated and paid the ransom, others would re-target the victim for another attack.

Michael knew to never surrender. His plan was not to attack back or build more firewalls, but to send the attackers off in other directions. He, along with his team, put forth a strategy, executed the tactics, and was successful in thwarting each attack and many others in the future. The name of the project? Dodge and Parry. This is a sword fighting technique thousands of years old. First fighters learn to simply move away or dodge an attack. Then they learn to parry, which is using a sword to deflect an attack. When properly executed the Dodge and Parry technique exhausts opponents until their weaknesses are revealed. Cardinal became so outstanding at Dodge and Parry that Michael considered applying for an additional internet patent with that name!

CHAPTER 6

Credit Shakespeare &
The Head of Goliath

We have nothing to sell but ourselves.

Part I—Debits and Credits

From a comfortable deep pool of water, then on a long dangerous journey, the best entrepreneurs instinctively swim upriver, against the strong currents of both time and place. Anyone who studies entrepreneurship recognizes this universal axiom. Entrepreneurs understand that swimming against the mainstream may lead to a successful spawning of their new ideas, potentially viable new concepts. But herein lies the mystery: What streams lead to fertile breeding beds of cool waters and what streams just lead to hot, shallow mud holes of death?

If we look back a few hundred years to a playwright who is often quoted for his wisdom and wit, we find a 16th century concept about wealth and society. William Shakespeare never realized how he submerged a monetary philosophy in the psyche of the Western world with just a few lines of prose. But that's exactly what he did. His words became a major tributary for wealth creation for strong swimming American entrepreneurs as far back as 1791, when the U.S.'s first Secretary of the Treasury, Alexander Hamilton, faced the same conundrum that all bankers, or "keepers of wealth," have struggled with since the beginning of time. Who exactly is a good bet for paying back a loan? With interest, of course.

First, let's look at Shakespeare and the expression that permeated fiscal policy for nearly 400 years. In Act I, Scene III of William Shakespeare's play, "Hamlet," Polonius counsels his son Laertes before he embarks on his visit to Paris, France. He says, "Neither a borrower nor a lender be; / For loan oft loses both itself and friend." Brilliant, short and sweet. Clearly Polonius, regarded by many as a fool, was nothing of the sort.

Polonius rightly understood that money changes everything in a relationship. When we borrow money from a friend, we may take advantages that may not be otherwise available. Eventually we face the ultimate humiliation: If we lend money, the pressure is reversed, and our friend most certainly will take the easy path and avoid paying back the loan. Eventually we lose our friend and our money. This may be why interest rates apply.

Michael, like Shakespeare, saw debt in two ways, not just one. Debt was on both sides of the same coin. In essence, there was no tail side to debt, just heads. First, he saw how debt focused him, his company, and his board members. They were all reminded frequently that this long journey upstream can lead to the cool waters for successful breeding. But debt also was used as a trigger for the credit card companies to make real money as they provide service.

> Cardinal provides access to a new source of wealth not imagined before. The individual demanded this access as they wanted and needed to be authenticated for the merchant.
> —Michael Keresman, 2007

One coin! Debt on both sides! Cardinal flipped the coin and won every time. If you think about it, eventually CardinalCommerce and intelligent authentication became the stream to give life.

Credit cards developed into the essential revenue stream, or life blood, for all of the big banks in the U.S. starting in the 1950s. Those banks that embraced the consequences of losses, hassles, lawsuits, bankruptcies, patent infringements and even fraud were eventually rewarded. Frankly, most people today have no idea just how long and hard the banks worked to create credit card lending. However, by the late 1960s these banks became the leaders of growth in America. Then, through example, America taught the rest of the world how to leverage customers for future financial expansion. The old world of "never a borrower nor lender be" was traded back. And now it is being supplanted again by intelligent authentication.

Consumers have new and different ways to pay for essential and non-essential wants and needs. Banks, merchants, and even tech companies are trying to protect their roles as platform facilitators for everyday purchases by offering more buy-now-pay-later options. Michael saw consumers as small, short-term bets or loans for everyday purchases. Little did he know hundreds of new companies from the financial tech industry, better known as "fin-tech," would hatch from his beautiful breeding pool of clear water.

With increased payment options for consumers, merchants would now finance more sales with less risk and add a new revenue stream as some consumers forgo credit-card purchases altogether. The two largest credit card companies would eventually own the delivery systems for the merchants as these point-of-sale options became consolidated.

Visa, Mastercard, American Express and others, which traditionally processed transactions between banks and retailers, made money by charging consumers interest and retailers a fee for in-store and online purchases. By getting into the point-of-sale lending business, these same firms could be the direct link between merchants and consumers, taking a percentage of the loan for individual transactions. Essentially, Michael saw CardinalCommerce facilitating loans directly between consumer and retailer. What happened next is a miracle in my mind. The lender would email the consumer the terms and conditions and information about repayment, all digitally with multiple credit options for a purchase with one, streamlined application. It is indeed a binary world.

Do you find it interesting that the millennial customers are turning out to be more like "the greatest generation" when it comes to debt? They are fundamentally distrustful of the traditional banking system, and for good reason. Both saw a near collapse of the financial world at a very impressionable time in their lives. Plus, aren't we all tired of hidden fees! So many ads today say NO HIDDEN FEES!

Fin-tech is happy to lure any and all investment opportunity with the new POS products and lending startups. They boast transparency! And you can take that all the way to the bank!

The New Cardinal Sales and Marketing

Today, the whole mindset behind sales has been turned on its head! Is everything a commodity now? The answer to this question is YES, but . . . . The but is, if and only if, we know for certain, exactly what we need well in advance. It's called supply and demand for a reason.

In addition, for anyone who works in sales, it is understood that there are three outcomes at the end of any sales pitch. YES, NO, or MAYBE. (That is, yes, they will buy, or no they will not buy, or maybe they will buy.) However, the real sales professional knows that the "sales dance" started long before that moment. Usually we hear a disingenuous "Can I help you find something today?" or "Is there something specific you are looking for?"

The internet has completely disrupted this tried and true method for sales. Methods cultivated and refined for the last 600 generations are now being rewritten with the new laws of the internet. Still, how could CardinalCommerce, a company formed at the time of the new millennium, wait until 2012 to build a 'real' sales force? How did Cardinal survive all those years with no substantial sales or sales force in place? Something must have changed the mindset in Michael Keresman long before Cardinal got to that moment.

Well for starters, Michael always anticipated that getting to the next level in business with intelligent authentication was going to mean CardinalCommerce needed to look equivalent to a traditional company, especially with the conservative and vibrant board members he cultivated. At least Cardinal needed a few of the departments found in any "normal" business. Arguably, building an intellectual property business is different, but having a sales department was still necessary. Michael will say that "at first Cardinal had nothing to sell but itself." Nonetheless, Michael hired a couple of distinguished people for "sales." But let's be clear, Michael was the sales force for CardinalCommerce. Sure, there were other individuals, but most employees worked across other company disciplines to help out. Perhaps it would be best to say that sales at Cardinal was business development that turned into customer relations that turned into customer service. Michael trained everyone, for the most part. Plus, with new IP products and enhancements that were so systemic to technology, management needed to cultivate sales talent from inside its own four walls. Mostly, Michael was constantly on the prowl to convert some guy or gal from a techie, geek position into a sales associate. Mr. Keresman pointed out in 2018, "Most people will say they hate sales. They say it's being deceptive. Then they say, the only way they would sell anything, would be if they actually believed in, or truly needed, the product. Well, there you have it. If you are building a product, day to day, I certainly hope you believe in that product."

Michael always assumed that before you can sell any bibles you have to have believers in religion itself. Once Michael had you interested in religion, selling the bible would be a breeze. That's how he would mold these pliable individuals into awesome representatives. They could easily administer customer service for each separate product line. This went on for many years. However, when 2012 rolled around, the Cardinal board, and even many shareholders, were completely committed to the concept that new capital should be infused to accelerate growth. This came in the form of adding seasoned marketing professionals. Finding trained sales experts in technology with real track records with established companies actually became a full-time job for Michael.

And another issue: Where will Michael find the funds? New capital for his little dream, CardinalCommerce, has been hard-earned. Well, Michael started right there in Cleveland, Ohio. The buzz all over town at that time: Cardinal was ready to hit the mother lode. So of course, his old friends at Primus Capital tried to contain themselves as they cut to the head of line for a piece of the pie. Michael didn't even have to finish his two-hour presentation to the principal owners at Primus. They knew it was an easy bet for their private equity firm. Millions of dollars poured in. Now Michael was really close to being totally self-actuated as an entrepreneur. Endorsements and accolades abound for our visionary entrepreneur. Yes, Michael was very close indeed. Private equity is a game of ego, bravado, and guts. Just a few years before, Michael could hardly get a return call from any of these firms that specialize in funding. In fact, Michael endured snickers or polite smirks, as cold shoulders turned away when socializing. Now quite suddenly he heard, "How can we get in line for all that money you are going to make us?"

Tara Lavelle, 3D Secure

The next step for Cardinal was clear. This is revolutionary business software with groundbreaking marketplace commerce solutions. They needed EXPOSURE! Enter Tara Lavelle, Senior Marketing Director for Cardinal from 2011 to 2020. Her initial message was nothing short of brilliant.

Once they had Rules-based Authentication, Tara easily claimed for anyone who would listen: "Yes, CardinalCommerce has developed Rules-based Authentication, and yes, we agree 3D Secure is cumbersome, but CardinalCommerce is not 3D Secure. CardinalCommerce is a service over 3D Secure that makes 3D Secure unobjectionable in all online transactions." Tara delivered this message at industry conferences, like Money 20/20, and in AdWords and so many other industry magazines, too. Issuing bank reps were overjoyed with extra security Cardinal could deliver! Re-positioning CardinalCommerce was a full-time job and Tara performed marvelously! Also, it should be pointed out, Tim Sherwin was instrumental in bringing Tara to Michael and CardinalCommerce in the first place.

> After we added Tara and a few key executives and the necessary personnel resources within the perspective domains, we began to see an immediate creation of new wealth from the backlog of sales inquiries. Frankly, we accelerated by tenfold in one year.
> —Michael Keresman, 2018

Michael relentlessly focused his team on development, operations, and customer services. Plus, the selling of business groups that were established over the last decade (merchant services, financial institutional services, and strategic alliances) all played into the theme Cardinal established.

Frankly, Cardinal had reached that point where it had finally proven its capabilities. Internet commerce was absolutely real. It was well over two decades from when Al Gore watched innocently from the White House as others labored for the first real "payment" on the internet.

Simultaneously, and as far back as 2008, Michael sensed a new assertiveness from the marketplace. Michael listened to the seismic

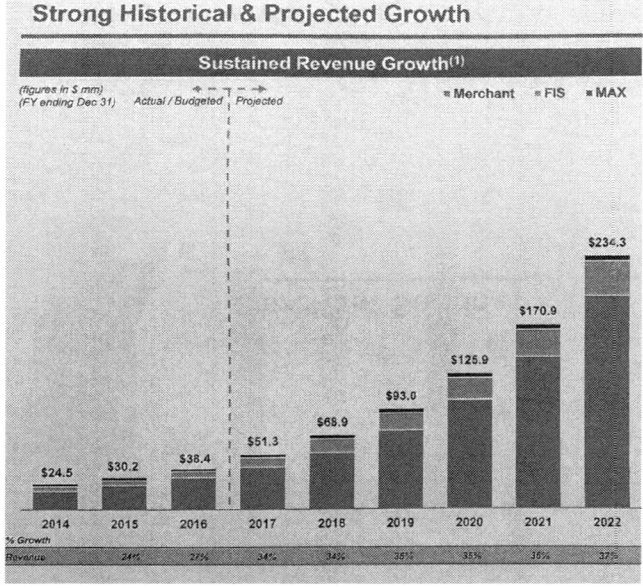

shift in attitudes from his executive colleagues, independent from the technology world. For instance, this scenario might present itself while on golf excursions with friendly business owners and executives. Michael eavesdropped on conversations as his top executive friends pondered the expanding of their corporate executive suite. To be exact, they needed to expand their corporate suite to include a new internet Commerce Division. Basically, to be forward-looking in e-commerce, their human resourcing needed to change to a modern world. Michael might have heard how various companies were starting their board meetings by discussing the new sectors and markets that internet sales has opened. As opposed to four or six years prior, when the e-commerce division for the vast majority of the corporate world was nothing more than a few college-level interns three or four levels down. They weren't even invited to board meetings. What for? The internet was inconsequential to the bottom line. Now all of a sudden, these companies had an internet executive. Often, this person was called the Experience Manager. Then within a few years, this Experience Manager would be leading presentations in board rooms of Fortune 500 companies! All of a sudden, the online experience was critical to every company's brand. Did intelligent authentication create all this too?

This new attitude resonated with the marketplace, and the demand for CardinalCommerce was for more than just a boutique company. Visa, Mastercard and the other card companies realized, quite selfishly, they too needed innovative service technology software—the kind of technology CardinalCommerce created a decade earlier. This was imperative for their future. These firms had a decision to make: Do they make it themselves or buy it? Buying it would have certain advantages; making it themselves would have different advantages.

In fact, Mastercard and Visa had already anticipated this shift. In 2003 and 2004, anti-trust murmurings were becoming more frequent. Customers and governments alike were more than curious. Just who exactly was paying the bills? The solution was simple. It was time to go public. Independently, both card companies eventually knew it was best to let everyone have a chance to be a shareholder. However, that is easier said than done! How does one go public with a multinational conglomerate corporation?

The card companies desired more independence from the consortium of banks they represented because being in a confederation of banks all around the world was starting to work against them. Going public, accordingly, was touted as a way to provide better service to the banks. So why was going public necessary? Regulations! Evolving into a service business, Visa / Mastercard can be light-footed without the burden of regulatory microscopes every day. Here, once again, bank regulations from governments add higher costs and longer intervals for necessary improvements and change. So, to be more transparent, they became less transparent?

As we know, the status quo finds new ways to preserve its wealth and power with barriers or hurdles. Banks are always under extra scrutiny for this very reason. Plus, remember that with the dawn of PayPal, many other payment service companies were trying to get in the game, too. Visa / Mastercard had to change, and they knew it.

Let's go back to something Michael said years ago in 2004 at an industry trade show called Money 20/20: "Imagine tens of thousands of banks, millions of merchants and billions of consumers all over the world! We must be able to trust one another for e-commerce to work."

Prophetic! This was the Cardinal business plan in two sentences!

Money 20/20 is a world class payments and fin-tech industry trade show in Las Vegas. It draws just the big wigs—Visa / Mastercard, Bank of America, Google, Cisco, etc.— with guest speakers like Ernest Garcia of Carvana and Robert Harjevec and Mark Cuban from "Shark Tank."

On this occasion, Michael delivered this now celebrated statement to an array of impressive colleagues and industry insiders. The moderator of the forum was the President and CEO of Mastercard. When the question of "trust" was introduced by Michael, the moderator scoffed and bristled at Mr. Keresman. Many of us would have been insulted. Not Michael Keresman. Especially when the elites of the current status quo are involved, Michael stands confident and devoid of ego or emotion. Once again, Michael is at his best when no shame interferes with vulnerability. Regardless, this executive felt the need to embarrass Michael with a snickering reply. "Maybe we all could get somewhere, if you guys in technology would stop talking about fraud, there is no fraud in payments!" What? No fraud? Remember this was the status quo in 2004. This is noteworthy because in just four years, her credit card company needed brand loyalty more than ever. Here is why.

Visa, Mastercard, and American Express are among the greatest brands in the world. But if your brand doesn't work, that's a problem. Visa had to evolve to services, either directly or indirectly. It needed to provide associated services to ultimately enhance its brand. Frankly, the card companies could not afford anything condescending about their brands whatsoever. Just as small Bank XYZ's brand is very important, too. It must also be able to say: When you use Bank XYZ, "we" can assure you safety, security, no fraud, no cumbersome extra steps, and high acceptance rates. Here the "we" is Visa and small Bank XYZ working together. However, when PayPal surfaced, it provided a direct connection to the customer's checking account. Radical ideas bloomed in the fin-tech world. Hundreds of new innovative companies followed. Conversely, it is important to understand that the vast majority of PayPal transactions are just a Visa or Mastercard anyway.

It's interesting that after the dot com bubble in 1999, as a country we created supplementary wealth because of the internet. It seems the cool waters for successful spawning were just around the next bend after all. Without a doubt, Visa / Mastercard and the others take brand erosion very seriously. In the USA, we actually have a "Cut Up Your Credit Card Day." It's October 16.

But we should also remember that when Visa went public in 2008, we were in the midst of one of the largest downturns in modern economic history. Often referred to as "the great recession," this global crisis in capital liquidity began much earlier, in 2007. Visa's IPO price was near $40 when offered. The company sold 406 million shares in the offering, raising just under $18 billion. That far surpassed the $10.6 billion AT&T Wireless IPO in 2000, previously the biggest U.S. initial offering.

Do you think Michael's little lawsuit in Australia may have had an effect on the direction Visa took thereafter? Michael and his dream, CardinalCommerce, against the limitless giant Visa. But to be fair, Mastercard had already seen the tea leaves of change. Mastercard went public first, in 2006.

Takeaways:

1. You have to be strong to swim against the mainstream
2. Do you know how your company appears to others?
3. How are your peers accessing your industry?
4. Make a business plan in one or two sentences
5. The keepers of the status quo may be ignorant, but they were first for a reason

Part II—The Head of Goliath

By 2010 Tim Sherwin and Michael Keresman knew more about crafting strategic partners than just about anyone in the fin-tech ecosphere. They knew everyone! Lest we forget, Chandra was a walking encyclopedia on the capabilities of all the technology related to payments. As influencers, the Cardinal team were second to none. Influence is often associated with momentum. And in business, momentum is everything. How would Michael deal with the momentum of his business that would lead to the desired liquidity outcome for CardinalCommerce, and, how did he know when?

Michael points to his tenure at STERIS. He pointed out that companies like Colgate Palmolive, Kimberly-Clark, and Procter & Gamble were always interested in owning shares, or for that matter, owning the whole companies, that directly influence their brands. In fact, at that time, minimally invasive procedures were nearly 65% of the health care industry market. Medical device manufacturing was booming in the late 1970s all the way up to the early 1990s. However, most markets seem to expand to the same situation every time—both saturated and overpriced. Naturally these conglomerates always need to put their capital to work. If they cannot find a reasonable deal on the instrument side, then what's the closest thing? The service side. They found STERIS. Remember that STERIS reprocessed, or sterilized, the instruments used in health care. The argument is eternal: How do mature companies avoid capital stagnation? Today giant companies redistribute high concentrations of their capital on the influencers for the future growth of their products. Michael used this same concept when looking for a strategic partner for CardinalCommerce.

For some time now, the payments industry had been in a mini-golden age. From 2011 to 2020 more capital has been raised in fintech than any other facet of the world. This is very understandable. To outsiders it's quite attractive: recurring revenue, high growth, typically internet related, and/or mobile commerce related, too. This is sexy stuff! Tim, Chandra and Michael would hear all the time, "I like Cardinal's platform and technology, someday we will have to buy you guys." This statement, and 50 others just like it, was repeated over and over again. This is how banking and huge internet CEOs solve their problems. They buy it. However, Tim, Chandra and Michael would always respond the same way. CardinalCommerce was not for sale, until it was.

How to know when? When do you take the sword from the giant and cut off the head? Michael would say, "You better do it before the Philistine warrior wakes up." Because remember, in the biblical story, the stone thrown from David's slingshot only knocked Goliath unconscious.

Well, one of the stones Michael threw from his slingshot was insti-tuted very early in his business plan. It's called employee stock options. Michael made sure all of his employees had a vested interest. Another stone: Michael made sure that the Cardinal technology was inexorably tethered to Cardinal's highly specialized intellectual knowhow. And yet one more, Michael ensured that a certain number of high-profile summer internships resulted in a successful job offering. Frankly, Michael believes the finest compliment that can be made about any company is when top quality graduate talent returns to work for that company. Michael always loved that Cardinal attracted talent. These stones would be paramount for whatever deal was developed. Michael points out, "Sometimes things happen. Maybe an employment con-tract goes south or there is a lawsuit liability pending." How many adjustments were made after the deal was signed? Michael's answer was startling: zero. Post deal—zero adjustments. Zero. Michael said, "Actually, I don't know of any case where that's happened. I talk to people that have done countless more deals. Their response, 'There is always something that comes unwound at the end.' Yes. Cardinal was a clean deal."

Michael worked with several investment bankers over the years and here is the response from his investment banker for the Cardinal deal. "We've bought a lot of companies and we've also looked at buying a lot of companies and it isn't even close. Cardinal by far was the clean-est, most straightforward from a due diligence standpoint that we ever looked at."

Well one thing is certain, Michael knew if he sought liquidity, he must have the house in order. Literally, the physical house must be fresh and clean! People forget, after the new capital was infused in 2012, Michael moved the whole operation almost immediately to a new facility. Michael's goal was simple. When suitors would come to visit, he wanted to hear this (and by the way, this is exactly what he heard), "Google's got nothing on CardinalCommerce. Even 'we' don't have a facility nearly as high tech and oriented to the future as what Cardinal has here in Ohio. This place feels like the future of payments. It's wonderful." Please note, Michael designed the interior himself. Remember, when given a task, get out of the way. Let's look inside.

Cardinal's office is a large open floor plan with a one vast public area in the middle. This center of the building feels like the heart of the company. From here everything radiates out. Actually, hallways are not visible from here. Positioned near the middle are large communal stations or work pods. Some workstations were like awkward shaped caverns. They were mostly spherical with seating options molded into the bulwarks. White board walls were there for doodling and brain-storming. In other areas around the large complex, the ceiling seemed to disappear into a darkness. Here, because of the lighting, focused beam spotlights, the feeling changed to something more dramatic.

Then at the far end was a huge lunch area with a high-end restaurant style kitchen. Should Michael want or need a guest chef to appear, he had the perfect environment for a companywide meal and gathering. Plus, the executive suites and the board room could be sequestered from the rest of the building with separate entrances. Certain activities could happen without necessarily disturbing the rest of the company. All the offices that needed privacy had doors, but the walls were glass. Except for the space pods in the middle, the whole facility is layered in both warm and cool earth tones. For the conservative Cleveland, even in the tech sector, it feels like a close encounter of the nerdy kind.

Still, the big question: How do you know when to market the busi-ness as a whole? Michael went to his board. It was 2015. Cardinal rev-enues and projections were going through the roof. Michael asked if anyone would be disquieted if he called in the investment bankers to look over the possibility of a sale. All were content. It was Michael's baby anyway. Companies like Cardinal don't just put a "For Sale by Owner" sign out on the lawn. A month later, at the next board meeting Michael had a private list of 30 prospective buyers. Tim, Chandra, and a few others were asked to render opinions in the process. Michael decided to call this operation "TYCHE", after the mythological Greek goddess for prosperity and good fortune. No one knows for sure how divine intervention works anyway. So, TYCHE it is. To everyone else at the company, it was just another silly phrase from Mr. Keresman. One employee, Nikko Scaife, said, "When Mike is involved, sometimes you have no idea what he's talking about. But this time, with 'TYCHE' I knew it meant something super important." It would take months for the rest of the folks to discern the true meaning of the phrase.

Tim and Chandra, the co-founders of CardinalCommerce, worked

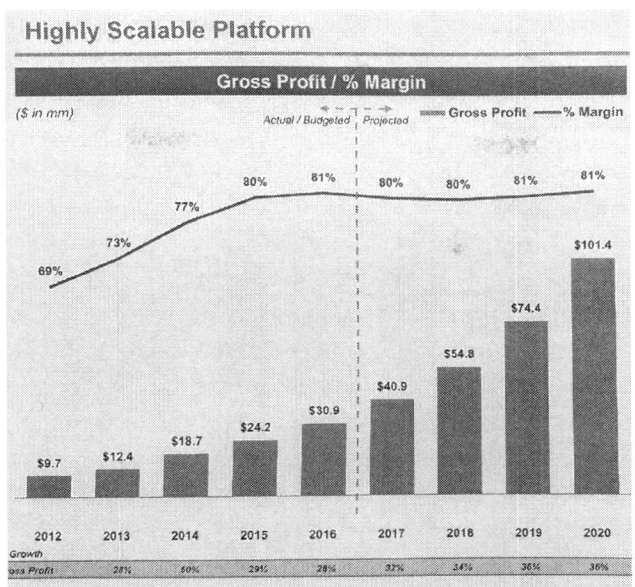

diligently, some might say relentlessly, to propel Michael's dream for a very long time. Now they were asked to help sell it. They didn't even blink an eye! That is loyalty.

Both Tim and Chandra, independently, had one buyer on their list that they knew would be a perfect fit. Not only that, Tim and Chandra secretly admired the swag this 'perfect fit' company presented to the rest of the world. Regardless, the master list was cut to 20 and then to 15. The investment bankers started to work on confidentiality agreements to flush out interested "Strategic Partners." At the end of the next month about five disinterested parties sent in their notice. They were eliminated from the list by their own choice. The list was down to about 10.

Tours were organized for the would-be suitors. Operation TYCHE was in full swing. I will use a football analogy here. Michael called simple plays; short passes and off tackle runs were very effective. Michael's team moved the ball upfield with ease. They overwhelmed everyone with efficiency, not flamboyancy. Tim and Chandra were having the time of their lives. Sure, they still had their regular work duties, but now they could rub elbows with some of their favorite industry insiders; all the gossip of "who's zooming who." (Please note, this phrase actually meant something completely different than it does today.)

Regardless, Michael just knew it was time. How? How did he know when Cardinal should be sold? Well for starters, Michael saw it in the eyes of his Best Man, Tim Sherwin. Remember, Michael never forgot what it was like to work as the "second in charge" at STERIS. Bill Sanford was a wonderful friend and a terrific leader. Heck, Bill was a staunch supporter of Cardinal from the beginning. Still, Michael knew back then almost 20 years ago, that one day he was going to be the real boss, the head honcho, the ringleader, the impresario! And that meant it was time for Tim to have that same opportunity, too. And Chandra also. Michael had pushed these men hard. They responded perfectly for 17 years! After all the due diligence and company tour whirlwind was over, the team cut the list to five. And guess what? Both Tim's and Chandra's #1 was still on the list!

NA / Not Applicable

Let's remember one of the requirements Michael projected of any potential strategic partner was to present a deal with certainty. In order for that to happen extensive due diligence would be performed by the last five potential buyers. Keep in mind when Cardinal was sold, Michael had between 170 and 180 employees. I asked Michael about the process suitors use for due diligence. Michael said there are long lists created by attorneys and managers that include the scrutinizing of Cardinal's personnel agreements, contracts, historic and pending lawsuits and any other legal proceedings. Basically, they are paid to turn over every stone. Here is what I find fascinating about Cardinal and a feature so unique to Michael's brand of entrepreneurship. Please note this may not be advisable to those of you who are thinking about starting your own business, but it's one I will always remember.

I said to Michael, it must have taken forever for each potential buyer to go over all the agreements and contracts, etc. Michael just smiled and said, "Nope not at all." This is why. When Michael had to check the boxes for what would be included in his electronic missives back to the strategic partner it was one big—NA / Not Applicable.

Employee handbooks: NA

Employee 'employment' agreements: NA

Employee regulations: NA

Executive 'employment' agreements: NA

Board servicing agreements: NA

Employee (all types) lawsuits: NA

Disgruntled employee legal actions: NA

Other legal, other than anything involving patents: NA

The only formal agreement Cardinal required with its employees was their respective stock option agreement. When Visa was preforming due diligence, one executive commented, "Do you mean to tell me, you guys just trust each other?" Michael answered, "That's how I built Cardinal—with trust."

The investment bankers established the last day of September 2016 as the official deadline for all serious offers. Michael remembered, after they received the offers, he started a financial matrix to weigh all the odds and ends of each deal. He wanted to have a dependable probability ratio for every contingency. He needed a number in his head on the odds. These are the odds of winning the biggest game of his life. Remember the very first "productivity model" he conjured so many years ago at HealthAmerica? Well, it was underway one last time. He was making those calculations when it hit him. Each strategic partner had unique approaches for its due diligence process. Maybe Michael could find some covert meaning in the individualized methods used? That's when the curtain was pulled back. Undeniably, one company stood far beyond the others when it came down to how they treated, or maybe we should say how they accepted the CardinalCommerce way; how they looked at Cardinal's market share; how they scrutinized the Cardinal IP and innovations; how they talked with all of the Cardinal employees! Actually, how they embraced Michael.

> Whatever profession you are engaged in, there is always one ultimate affirmation just waiting to be confirmed.
> —Michael Keresman 2018

It was time to choose one of the five. Tim, Chandra, and Michael collectively decided that Visa would be best suited to propel

CardinalCommerce forward. Michael set the price. This would be the price for exclusivity with Visa. Of course, Tim and Chandra knew it was Visa all along. They had Visa #1 on their list for a very long time!

It was then Michael allowed his mind to ponder the logistics in closing a deal of this magnitude with, of all companies in the world, Visa. Every employee and shareholder stock arrangement, all the vendor deals, routing numbers, escrow accounts, getting this transaction done was going to be a full-time job!

And then Michael learned not everything is as tidy for TECHY as he wanted. TECHY was Michael's codename for finding a strategic partner.

It seems there was a problem with the European Patent Office. While cleaning up some odds and ends Michael learned the European Patent Office (EPO) denied a patent for Cardinal's Universal Merchant Platform. This is crazy. This is the cornerstone of Cardinal's patents. And what was the problem? The EPO said the grounds for denial was based on its opinion that Cardinal's patent wasn't "technical."

With any governing body, there's usually an appeal process. Michael knew there was one last move possible. The European process tolerates a six-month appeal window. The Cardinal attorneys advised Michael to wait. There was no need to rush into anything! They said, with an open patent application, potential suitors like Visa would assume the patent was real. Michael thought, this was the prudent strategy. Appealing to the EPO at the last possible moment would be the path of least resistance.

But Michael would have nothing to do with it. Michael found his trusty sling shot. He had but two stones left in his pouch. Michael always believed Cardinal had satisfied the requirements for a European invention, and business method patent. These are the entrepreneurial nuances that so few of us posses. He summoned his best and most experienced technical personnel and posed a challenge to them. Basically, Michael explained that the EPO didn't believe the developments that Cardinal created were technical. Of course, you can easily imagine how Michael would have inspired the team to work night and day to prove there was technology involved in the creation of its Universal Merchant Platform.

Now armed with Cardinal's official findings, Michael directed the patent attorneys to press the final authority of the tribunal of judges for a hearing as soon as possible. Michael saw no reason to wait. Again, his attorneys only saw a downside. A downside with huge repercussions should they be denied. Laugh now if you like. Shortly after the formal appeal process was completed, Cardinal's European patent council called Michael. They informed him that the appeal was successful, and Cardinal was granted a business method patent for all of Europe. Yes, indeed the Universal Merchant Platform was a true piece of software technology. Most of us would have been thrilled, but not Michael. He wanted more. Michael wanted to know, when was the last time a patent process such as this concluded successfully by an inventor from outside the EU? As it was told to me, apparently, the judges from the tribunal looked at each other and simply said, we don't remember if there ever was such a case. Imagine that, our David and another successful conquest.

Let's just say, Michael penned the Visa exclusivity agreement with no fear. Please note, two weeks later, the Cleveland technology firm, the one not in Silicon Valley, known all over the world as CardinalCommerce, received the Visa reply. Visa accepted Michael's terms with zero contingencies. Unbelievable!

I asked Michael what Visa thought about Cleveland. This was Michael's hometown, the home of so many legendary businesspeople and industry moguls who built free enterprise. Cleveland is the place for groundbreaking entrepreneurship for over 150 years. Please remember, one of Michael's lifelong goals for Cardinal was to do something striking for Cleveland, Ohio. Here is what Michael said: "In Silicon Valley, it's quite common to see a constant shuffling of the deck or the pirating of high skilled labor and executives. Nonetheless, Visa loved the stickiness of the employees and their compensation levels I established here." Michael said jokingly, "We got nerds, really talented ones. But our nerds are married with kids, living in affordable, comfortable homes. Our nerds don't want to move. They like Cleveland. And now so does Visa." Frankly, I don't think Visa ever considered moving CardinalCommerce, not even once.

Michael set the closing for Jan. 31. That meant that on Feb. 1, 2017 Visa would own CardinalCommerce. Hundreds of stockholders waited anxiously that Wednesday. I doubt a single employee worked whatsoever. Once the money started flowing into each shareholder account, the way the deal was written, Visa had zero ability to pull it back. Unless some hoax or fraud was perpetuated, this was a one-way street.

Michael remembers the day was mostly surrealistic. "I was stunned this really happened. At the moment I felt self-actualized, professionally, and I thanked the Lord! I did it. When I say, 'did it,' I don't want to omit anybody's contribution. However, along the way, many people snickered, some even laughed, and a few ridiculed me behind my back. I took the chance to do this, and I never wavered in my conviction. Then on that Wednesday when the bank was sending notifications about the transfers, in that one moment . . ." Michael stopped talking, nothing but dead silence. Is the interview over? No, I could feel his emotion. Michael needed to gather himself here. I had seen this heart stopping vulnerability one time before at Lake Erie College. Michael started up again. "I don't know . . . maybe . . . well, I've never won a Super Bowl. But I think there must be an elegance when the final seconds tick off the clock and the next thing you know you are a Super Bowl champion forever."

I felt a slight burning in my nostrils and my eyes became misty. Michael's deep affection for free enterprise, commerce and entrepreneurship and the rewards felt by the individual and the collective is simply overwhelming. It's just business, right? Michael gracefully continued his thought.

He modulated his voice to accommodate the obvious emotion he was experiencing. "There are a few average athletes that become Super Bowl champs. Conversely there are thousands of really hard-working players, really talented men who never appeared in a single Super Bowl game. Truthfully, we won the Super Bowl. Only it wasn't a season, one endeavor, it was multiple years. Everything just, pow, a lot of tension and anxiety, a lot of frustration, and a lot of 'everythings' just melted away. And I remember thinking to myself, 'Thank God this happened and that I'm no longer important.'" Michael never once talked to me this way before. I was astonished at his self-effacement. Who is this guy? Where did the strong, confident and honorable Michael go? He was still there! We both took a moment and a few deep breaths.

Michael had more to say. I listened. "I did not have to do any more professional engagements. No more presentations. I did not have to do anything more in my business life. There are people who do bigger deals. They're people who do more spectacular deals, but this was something I envisioned myself. We hit our mark a hundred percent. It was done. The idea of building a company from scratch in my hometown Cleveland, Ohio with the name of Cardinal, against all odds was instantly personified. Sure, I made enough, actually more than enough. It was a great deal for the stockholders, including the largest. It was a fantastic deal for the employees—Visa kept everybody. Actually, Visa corporatized benefits and perks and those kinds of things. Basically, everybody got a raise. And a great deal for Cleveland. Because the Greater Cleveland Growth Association, the City Chamber, all of the muckety-mucks that promote and attract businesses to our area can say that Visa, one of the most successful brands in the world, has a presence in my hometown Cleveland, Ohio. The dream came true; the Cardinal dream came true." I was dumbfounded, what a class act.

Michael remembers meeting Tim and Chandra in the board room later in the day. There was the usual champagne toast and the salutes, "We did it! We did it." Michael also remembers very well how much he trusted and loved these men, his Best Man and the Professor.

Takeaways:

1. Who are the industry influencers in your company?
2. Build towards zero liabilities or adjustments for a sale
3. Who in your industry can grant complete affirmation?

CHAPTER 7

Commencement Day

It's Saturday, May 19, 2018. It's a balmy 85 degrees outside, which is unseasonably warm for northeast Ohio. However, the breeze off Lake Erie is helping to cool down the afternoon somewhat. The Lake Erie College campus is teeming with the families and friends wishing to celebrate their loved one's time-honored tradition of receiving a college diploma. This commencement tradition has been conducted at this school for over 150 years. However, very few of these graduates are pondering the future with as much wisdom and insight as is Michael Keresman. Michael has been thinking about this day for some time now. Michael has been asked to be the keynote commencement speaker, and he can't wait to deliver his message. Candidly, he knows exactly what is going to happen to every student after today. Michael will be sitting on the dais with all the other school dignitaries pondering numbers yet again. Michael will play this game in his head to keep from getting nervous. Actually, Michael doesn't get nervous during speeches. Either way, Michael occupies his mind with numbers; always predicting outcomes. Michael will deliberate swiftly. This is how many graduates already have a job. This is how many have not. This is how many will go on to graduate school. This is how many will continue living at home. This is how many will be the first someone in their family to graduate from college. This is how many will be going into the military. This is how many will move away from Northeast Ohio. This is how many will move back. This is how many will go into banking, law, education, real estate, computer science, medicine, engineering, entertainment, transportation, conservation. This is how many have dogs, cats or lizards. All of these innocuous ideas will be whirling around in that brain of his.

Then Michael saves the best for last . . . And this is how many will become entrepreneurs. Michael just knows. He can look into the faces of these graduates and know which ones of these will meaningfully challenge themselves and others for a better world. These are the ones who ponder, "How is this world supposed to be?" He can spot them in three seconds. He knows how they feel. He knows how they think. He understands the drive, the desire and the dream they have of being an entrepreneur. Frankly, He's not here for them. He's here for everyone else.

Pondering the full life and career of Michael Keresman, what will he want to say? What will he want everybody at this commencement to know about him? What perspective will he want to resonate?

Here at the grand hall at Lake Erie College, there must be 1,500 people present, all for the same reason. A long stage sweeps across the entirety of the room from far left to far right. There are three rows of chairs comfortably placed for faculty and school dignitaries. There is one lonely podium that stands in the middle. Everyone knows, it's from here that everything must follow.

After the pomp, circumstance and ceremonial entrance of Lake Erie College's faculty, staff and trustees, the tradition comes to order with kind words and reflection by the highest-ranking college official, the president of the school, Dr. Brian Posler. In just a few moments Dr. Posler will happily introduce Michael Keresman to the audience and welcome him to the podium. Everyone knows what happens after that. Michael will say a few words and the diplomas will be handed out to the graduates.

Well, now is the time. Dr. Posler has finished. He turns towards Michael as a gracious round of applause echoes. Michael moves forward to the podium. The room becomes uncomfortably quiet. Down in the front row sits Michael's lovely wife Liz and family. Michael glances down to Liz and gives her a little wink. Michael then settles in with a warmth and assuredness that is hard to describe. Michael named his speech for Lake Erie College: "Something Important, Something Meaningful, Something to Remember." This is how it all played out.

At first, Michael paused, then he scanned the entire audience. He gratefully moved forward from there.

"I am told by others that have done this sort of thing, you know, 'commencement speeches,' that if I do a good job today, I will have 'said' something important; and I will have 'said' something meaningful; and I will have 'said' something to remember. So, if it's OK with you, here I go."

Michael cleared his throat. Again, he scanned the audience. He was really trying to build this moment up.

"OK, something important. OK, here I go."

He paused, then spoke very slowly.

"Something important."

Michael looked at the audience.

"Now something meaningful."

He paused.

"Something meaningful."

Again, he paused and looked out at the audience.

"And now for the tough one: something to remember."

Michael paused.

"Something to remember."

Michael proudly looked at his audience.

"There, I said all three," he announced, as if he was done with the speech.

"Oh, did a few of you miss that? I can do it again. Here, let me do that again."

Michael cleared his throat. Again he scanned the audience.

"Something important!"

Michael was stronger this time.

"Something meaningful!"

Even stronger.

"And I must not forget . . . *Something to remember!*"

The audience busted up laughing. In fact, a few claps could be heard from around the auditorium. Michael really enjoyed himself here. He was laughing along with them.

Then Michael waited for his audience to settle down again. Then he continued:

Well, right now I'm president of something called Three by Three

Ventures. And Three by Three Ventures means my wife Liz and I raised three wonderful children, three 'A-plus' girls. Also, we were a part of three successful ventures. As I stand here, and the older I get, when I look at the value of all those things, I think the first three were the more important. But I do want to talk about the other three ventures that I did too. The moral of what I'm going to tell you is that when you go out into the world, you are going to face odds against you. You're going to face disbelievers. And what you're actually going to find is you're going to face people that stick out their foot in hopes of tripping you up along your way. It's not because it's you, or because you're tall or short or anything personal like that. It's just the way it is because it's the status quo. You see, people have been known to make money on the status quo. We, you and I, have to break through the status quo to make our mark in the world. Here, let me explain.

The first venture I was fortunate enough to be involved with was to be a part of the management team of the first statewide health maintenance organization or HMO network in the country. I got this job, Group Health Plan of Northeast Ohio, which later was renamed HealthAmerica. Former governor of Tennessee, former mayor of Nashville, his name is Phil Bredesen, was the founder of that. So, when I got this, my first executive job, my mother had me over for a dinner. She was so excited; she wanted to give me a celebratory meal of sorts.

It was August in 1982 and I had been out of college for about three years. This was indeed an important job for many reasons, but most importantly, above all, I was hired to perform duties that were in my wheelhouse. My mind was on numbers, accounting 24/7. I just loved numbers, high-finance and business. To me it meant freedom. Numbers were liberating. When properly structured, numbers were like architecture; I could envision the whole building right before MY mind's eye. Just like we are here today in this historic building at this remarkable institution.

Michael gestured by swinging his right arm across his body. Again, he scanned the audience and continued,

I was so proud of my new employment, but not just because I was doing what I loved, working in accounting, but because I had finally "arrived." What does that mean, "I finally arrived?" To me, this job gave me the sense of being a real person; to work and get a paycheck to be a contributor of society. If nothing else, my mother and father taught me the value of a good work ethic. Also, this meant I was eligible for a "traditional family life." I could think about starting my own family.

Michael gazed right into the eyes of his loving wife Liz and then to each of his daughters. He continued,

I would be contributing to the good in society. It also meant owning nicer things and having bigger rewards, like a new car! "Arriving" has its rewards! However, my father had other thoughts on the matter, as I was soon to learn.

At my celebratory meal my mother had prepared my favorite meal, Chicken Paprikash. This was a lovely late summer evening for all concerned. In those days, it was customary for my father to move to the family room immediately after dinner. There he could relax a bit away from the kitchen area with a little after-dinner drink. He liked Manhattans. The TV could be heard faintly in the background. Lawrence Welk and his orchestra provided soft entertainment music for all of us.

So, I thought, I'm going to the family room to have an after-dinner drink with my father. We are going to talk about "men things." I'm no longer a kid. I knew all about important matters, politics, business or maybe even sports. My thoughts would be treated with equal weight and respect. After all, I'm my father's peer now. Maybe we could talk about General Motors vs. Honda. Or maybe we could talk about the baseball season. The Indians' new slugger, Andre Thornton, was a big star that year.

As I sat down, my father looked at me with concern. He said, "What the hell are you doing with that HMO—company? Tell me, son, what were you thinking when you took this career limiting job? I thought I taught you better than this. These people at HealthAmerica have not a clue. HMOs will never make it. Everybody uses Blue Cross and Blue Shield!"

Michael looked directly at the audience. He continued,

Well, as you might imagine, I was devastated. I thought, "I really earned this opportunity, and now my father is saying the exact opposite. Did I not deserve an executive role so soon after college? Or was he just attacking my employer, an HMO?" Maybe attacking my employer was his way to get the message across that I didn't earn this position. Actually, this conundrum sent my mind swimming.

Now Michael looked over the heads of the audience members. He was searching for something in the distance almost. The room was dead silent. He continued,

So, I did the only sensible thing I could muster. I got up, and thanked my mother for a lovely meal, and left. On the way to the door, my mother stopped me for a moment. She had heard what her husband, my father, had said. My mother said in a half whisper, "He has no idea what he's talking about. He doesn't pay the bills, I do. We haven't used Blue Cross for years." She then handed me a small gift. It was all wrapped up. She looked at me and said, "Either way, I'm proud of you, son." Inside was a bracelet with my initials. And the inscription underneath read; "To the man you've become—To the son you'll always be."

The audience was stunned. Michael looked at all the faces across the huge hall and continued,

So, facing the world, you would think your father would be your advocate, but my father thought I was wasting my time. And back then, HMOs were considered socialized medicine. Back in the 1980s about 5% of the country were covered by something similar to an HMO. Maybe not even that many! So, by the year 2000, 70% of the people in the country had some form of health insurance or managed care. Today, it's even higher and it's nearly all of the country. The point is, in the early days, it was nothing but an uphill battle. And I found out . . . that even your friends and family can discourage you.

So, the three real thoughts I want to leave you with today are these.

Michael became more animated. His pace and energy felt more uplifting. The audience was right with him. He continued,

Number one, you have to believe in yourself. There are going to be obstacles. You can point your fingers at all the reasons why they singled you out. But understand that thing, the status quo, is actually blind to who you are; it's actually deaf to who you are; and it's insensitive to who you are. Because they, the status quo, are doing their thing independent of you. It's OK to have that chip on your shoulder. It may motivate you. But recognize that the status quo is essentially deaf, dumb, and blind to who you are. Notice the words I chose: deaf, dumb and blind. You can blame them. It's because you're black and you're not getting the opportunity. You can blame them because you are a woman, and you can blame it on whatever you like. *But the truth is, they really don't know who you are.*

Number two, you are going to be filled with the domain of "what is." That status quo is going to tell you . . . how things are, and you have to challenge that.

When I was in sixth grade, I remember reading something called "The Weekly Reader." The big message in "The Weekly Reader" was how far behind the United States had fallen in building nuclear power plants. Back then, the environmentalists were insistent that the answer for the environment was nuclear power. That was the road to cleaner energy, and we had fallen far behind France because they had 47 nuclear power plants.

Now today, if you were to ask the environmentalists, they would not say nuclear power plants are the answer. So, the point is just because it's *contemporary and vogue,* and more and more people are *yelling loudly* about it, doesn't mean it's the right answer. In fact, with my experience and in my life, I find that most of the time the *loudest yellers are behind the wrong answer.*

So, what do we do?

Michael smiled at his audience.

"We should find out for ourselves," he continued.

Michael smiled warmly again. He paused to let his last statement resonate. He continued,

So, I don't know a damn thing about global warming. I'm not a scientist. I'm not a meteorologist. But what I can do is count. *In fact, I've been a good counter,* so I was looking for something I could *count* to help me understand this dilemma. What might give me some comfort one way or the other? So, I thought, what is the poster child for the global warming, the animal that appears on the poster or the image that we see for the global warming argument?—Polar bears! So, I Google how many polar bears are there?

Well, I can tell you that in 1950 there were 5,000 polar bears. And, today, there are too many to count. Experts estimate there are somewhere between 20 to 25,000. People in Iceland go on polar bear hunting parties because the polar bear is such a voracious predator. And, by the way, the natural burial location for polar bears . . . is the ice floe. The weaker ones that are challenging the status quo . . . They are pushed further and further out on the weakest ice. That's how it works.

Now, I don't know if that proves or disproves global warming. But what I do know is that polar bears are not in danger. The tie between polar bears and global warming may not be true if there are five times more polar bears now.

Michael slowed down for just a moment here. He looked at the podium and then he looked back at the audience.

Maybe that means a lot or maybe it doesn't. The point is, you are going to have to find out for yourself. Getting in the parade because everybody else is getting in that parade doesn't mean . . . it's the right parade. *Find out for yourself.*

Number three, you are going to run into a lot of opportunities in life: to make money, to enrich yourself, and to reach something we call self-actualization. *At the end of the day, however, you are going to have to find a way to be satisfied, truly satisfied.*

Part of that is how you live your life. Did you take a shortcut? Did you create more bridges than you tore down? We all can try and fix the world. There are a lot of people up here that can tell you how to fix the world, but I don't know how to fix the world. *In fact, I know I can't fix the world.*

What I can do is take life up close and personal. Did I make that relationship between you and me today better? Or worse? What I believe, if we concentrate far more on the up close and personal world . . .the one that is right there in front of us, and we do that a little better . . . *the other world will take care of itself.*

Stop trying to fix the world. Look closely at, *who you really are,* and what *you are doing to those around you. Concentrate more on the 'proximity relationships' and less on the esoteric relationships—that we probably and individually can do nothing about.*

Now it may not surprise you that the so called "King of Pop," Michael Jackson, is the number one downloaded artist/singer of all time. But it just might surprise you which tune of his is. Given the plethora of number one tunes he created; I find it interesting that the number one tune for downloads is 'The Man in The Mirror.'

There just might be more of a message here than you think. *Work on yourself, first.*

Michael looked at the audience and paused for just a moment. It was a little awkward. Actually, the intensity in the room seemed to increase. Michael had become emotional. Who in this audience is cognizant of what may be going on inside Michael's mind at this juncture in his life? To be on this platform, in front of all these people, these random nobodies. To know that virtually everyone there has no idea how their lives have changed, all because of what he and his team created! The magnitude of his vulnerability becomes unmistakable. The pause carried on for another moment. Then Michael broke the embarrassment rather quickly. Michael continued.

I just have one last thing I need to say.
I feel truly honored to be your guest.
And thank you for listening.

That was it! Fifty or more audience members jumped to their feet clapping wildly. He obviously made a connection with them. They were excessively enthusiastic. Plus, there were at least a half-dozen faculty members who did the same. All of these individuals were immediate with their fervor. A few of the graduating youngsters hooted and hollered to take the energy level and moment even higher. Then gradually of course, the rest of the audience respectfully stood up and continued the ovation for a comfortable length of time. Michael was so confident and vulnerable to his own emotions that day. It was a grand moment for Michael Keresman.

However, is this what you thought he was going to say to the audience that day? If you were Michael Keresman, is this even close to what you would have said? All of his accomplishments and the magnitude and repercussions of his groundbreaking concepts and ideas, and really, no details about e-commerce. Why? Maybe because Mr. Keresman is way more than a speculator or promoter. Maybe he's even more than a modern-day impresario. Maybe he's even more than an industry mogul. Michael honed and developed his skills over decades. Maybe Michael Keresman is nothing like us!

Federal Reserve of Northeast Ohio

Michael is a member of the Cleveland Business Advisory Council for the Federal Reserve Bank of Cleveland. He serves alongside 12 prominent business and political leaders. Terms are at the pleasure of the chairman and usually last four years. The Federal Reserve Council, Chapter Northeast Ohio, covers the entire state of Ohio, plus 56 counties in eastern Kentucky, 19 counties in western Pennsylvania, and 6 counties in northern West Virginia. Michael has just returned from its quarterly meeting that takes place in downtown Cleveland.

It's noon on Oct. 2, 2018. Michael has invited me for an impromptu lunch at the Kirtland Country Club. We are situated in Northeast Ohio at the foothills that lead to the Allegheny Mountains. This is one of the most beautiful golf courses in the Midwest. This is, without a doubt, Michael's favorite hangout now that he is retired. We are having a spectacular fall day. It's sunny and warm, with enormous white and gray clouds filling the sky. It's breezy, but I'm compelled to remove my sweater at any second. Gosh, I hope Michael invites me to play golf after lunch! It's on days like this I feel I could have a hole-in-one! That's how perfect this day feels. Please note, this interview is the remaining reason why I agreed to write this book. If you think you know Michael A. Keresman, wait until you read this interview. Michael finds me sitting at a table at the men's locker house. We order our lunch from the attentive waiter and I start asking questions. Michael seems especially open and receptive.

PATRICK: What can you tell me about today's Federal Reserve meeting?

MICHAEL: We were talking about the unemployment rate at the

Federal Reserve Advisory Council today. The Federal Reserve used 6% unemployment rate as a target for full employment. The mindset from The Federal Reserve; that's a job well done . . . 6% was good enough for the U.S. economy. The two goals of the Federal Reserve are to keep inflation away and work towards full employment, so I thought I would ask, what was their full-employment objective? And they said, "Well, we've lowered it to under 6%!" And I said, "Well that's not good enough."

(Michael explains there is a certain amount of unemployment not expressed in the percentages, for people switching jobs, currently furloughed, or transitioning because of life circumstances.)

You see, but what happens when we are in textbook, full employment? When we are anywhere above 4%, workers tend to become disenfranchised and stop looking for jobs. The participation rate falls. You see, when we push towards 3% and even lower, disenfranchised workers re-enter the workforce, and some of the people that had stopped participating begin to participate. Oftentimes, those are the lower-skilled workers, and historically they participate at a higher percentage of the unemployment rate. In my opinion, the feds should really aim for sub-3% rate when calculating unemployment. Then the participation rate goes to the point where it's saturated.

PATRICK: Who is chairman of this committee?

MICHAEL: The Chairman of the Federal Reserve Bank in Cleveland is Loretta Mester.

PATRICK: what did Loretta say?

MICHAEL: Well, she said there's some danger when you get to too many people employed. It starts to put pressure on inflation and higher wages. And I said, "Higher wages are a good thing." And Loretta said, "Only if the productivity keeps up or matches the wage." And I said, "No. In the short term it might not match. But what we find is employers figure out how to increase the productivity. You're always going to have technology help move to a more positive productivity. So, to some degree, the emancipation of the worker is a full-employed or underemployed economy. The employer is not more noble or virtuous, but they do understand employees are valuable. Since the beginning of time, we have seen that they'll figure out a way to increase their productivity, which always ends up with higher pay."

PATRICK: Always?

MICHAEL: Always!

MICHAEL: I noticed Loretta taking copious notes.

(Michael smiles to himself and looks away.)

PATRICK: Can you tell me what this smile means?

MICHAEL: she knows me well enough. I always have somewhat of a contrarian view, a different view than the Feds. It's enlightening to them because they don't hear this stuff. You see, they're stuck in a very analytical world, and nobody has better data than the Feds. But it's all empirical and quantifiable. They simply never get to digest "subjective information" and they need to, as much as they can. I mean, you've got to respect them, as they stay within "that band" of data. When you get outside of that band of data, eventually it will show up in a market, show up in statistics, but the lag time of that is significant. So, hearing a different perspective is important to them.

PATRICK: When did they ask you to be on this committee?

MICHAEL: So, I've had several terms, two-year terms. I believe once Cardinal was sold, I was no longer qualified. But they keep me on the committee anyway, probably because of my charm and good looks.

PATRICK: Who else is on the committee?

MICHAEL: I have a list I can show you, a couple of manufacturing companies, a software company, Hyland Software is on it, a guy who makes some video display stuff in Akron. He's very liberal, so we end up jousting on occasion.

PATRICK: Sounds less homogeneous than one might suspect?

MICHAEL: That's what they want. One guy is from a prominent head-hunting firm; he's kind of a leading indicator. "Is his demand up or down?" "Have wages been up or not?" You want different perspectives.

PATRICK: What is the basic meeting structure?

MICHAEL: the first half-hour, we go over the economy, all the different indexes and statistics for forecasting the economy. They have elaborate graphs, etc. With 16 federal reserve chairmen around the country, they love to chart where they think the economy is going six months from now, a year from now, two years, and even three years. The Fed is very accurate and comfortable reaching out a quarter. However, once they start going into a year, other factors and unforeseen consequences come into play.

PATRICK: Tariffs have been the hot topic for some time now. Did you ever bring up anybody that you knew that had any tariff issues at one of these meetings?

MICHAEL: Well, here is a story. There was a guy who was really getting the shortend of the stick because he uses China for his manufacturing. So, when the ships are already on the shore of an American dock, the manufacturer has already been paid. The U.S. companies have to pay the tariff. The Chinese don't pay. The American companies pay. So, he had to scurry and do some things because he was worried about going under. He doesn't really have a sense of these tariffs. "I don't really understand those tariffs." Yada, yada, yada. It goes on and on and on.

PATRICK: This is one of the guys of the Federal Reserve Committee?

MICHAEL: One of the guys on the committee, yes. We'd be listening to this for 10, 12 minutes. But other than just the first three minutes, it was a rehash. "I don't get these tariffs. I don't get these tariffs." However, one manufacturing company said, "By the way, what happened to you happened to one of our customers! Because they said they can't afford to shut down or pay more, they in-sourced to the United States what they normally would have bought from China. It created some jobs."

PATRICK: Immediately?

MICHAEL: Immediately. And the guy came back two weeks later to complain about that. I said, "Let's take a step back. And the assumption is that tariffs hurt. Keep in mind, this is designed to create tension, to force people to negotiate to get a better deal."

PATRICK: Are you always this bold?

MICHAEL: YES. I said these tariffs are designed to create tension, to bring negotiators a table to get a better deal. That resonated because it's nice to hear the other people say, "Yes, it's a negotiating ploy." So, what people aren't looking at with regard to tariffs, is China doesn't play fair. They never have. So, in China, before these tariffs' agreement, it was like having a hole in your boat. And as long as you have a hole in the boat, you're sapping and sucking out the productivity of America. China actually files an enormous amount of intellectual property in the United States, but we can't do the same there. Oh no, that wouldn't be right!

PATRICK: Does any of this effect Cardinal?

MICHAEL: Well, I said, as a matter a fact, I believe Alibaba was infringing on our patents.

PATRICK: Do they have some history of this?

MICHAEL: They always have. And the problem is, they can come here with plenty of legal representatives in the United States. They keep us from doing things, so we have to go through "due process." Who might indeed win that? But we couldn't attack them. So, that's part of the hole in the boat. Especially IP! (Intellectual Property) If you look back, it wasn't until the Vietnamese started stealing China's IP. That's when America woke up, when China came to the International Trade Organization. (Michael laughs!)

PATRICK: Is that funny?

MICHAEL: Well, everyone kind of chuckled that China was complaining about "cheaters." So, China has started to come to the table, but we still have a hole in the boat. For America, we have to plug that hole, otherwise it's just like exporting free dollars to China.

PATRICK: So, what else turned up in today's discussion?

MICHAEL: Mmm-hmm. We were talking about how to create a work environment for the millennials. The person from Hyland Software was saying, "A raise isn't going to change their mind to stay or leave the company. They're looking at the whole culture aspect: time off, flex time, etc. Believe it or not, with the 'Family Act,' there are men that take 12 weeks off to be with their wife and newborn child." And I said, "The husband? What does he do for 12 weeks?" I even said, "I don't get this." Oh, you could see the room start to stir, and a couple of the people started to chuckle. "They will bond, and they will do things with their peers from work. They tend to work in pods, and they might not have quite as strong a social life as other disciplines, so they tend to find their social life in work. And when I see one of these developers not interacting, that's a warning flag for us, because they tend to not stay. The people who interact with one another outside work tend to stay."

PATRICK: So, is this solving the millennial issue in today's working world?

MICHAEL: It is! But Hyland and Cardinal have had greater success by not hiring at the skill level needed. We tend to be more like a baseball team with a farm team. We bring people in right out of school. Maybe they're a history major, or a physics major, or whatever. Then they go into technology and they become quite valuable. So, for a while you're subsidizing for competence. Then everybody is getting a benefit because we are not paying for a racehorse when a mule horse will do just fine! (Patrick and Michael laugh.)

PATRICK: And those were real-world experiences you had at STERIS, also?

MICHAEL: Yes, and Hyland, and then the manufacturing guy says, "We do that too, but we'll bring people in, shipping guys, and pay for their education to be machinists. We're not paying machinists 70 grand a year and continually raise rates." So there is upper pressure on wages.

PATRICK: I recently heard a COO of a well-known construction company here in Lake County say, "There has never been a better time to enter the middle class than today."

MICHAEL: Absolutely. Well, I don't know about ever, but definitely in my lifetime. I would agree.

PATRICK: And he said, if you're willing to put in the 40 to 50 hours of "real work," you can get paid extremely well in today's climate.

MICHAEL: Yep. I agree with that. And you'll get better benefits than you ever did, more flex time, more free time, more vacation time.

PATRICK: Michael, how did this happen?

MICHAEL: I summed it up this way at the Fed meeting, saying that the emancipation of workers in a full-employment economy, and anything we do to not drive that unemployment rate down, flips the benefit to the employer. A full-employed economy, one that's over-heating, causes the employer to look at that resource called "human beings" as an asset! They have to take more care of that asset, developing that asset, enhancing their work experience because without that pressure of "I might lose that asset," you can have all the government programs on God's Green Earth and it will not have that same effect. In fact, it will have a counter-effect.

PATRICK: Did you say that today?

MICHAEL: I most certainly did. (Michael thinks to himself for a moment.) I don't think many of these people go to meetings like this, that are this energetic. It doesn't matter if they agree or don't agree or laugh or not.

PATRICK: So, this is a very entertaining meeting?

MICHAEL: What I do is fun. Well, first of all, it's intellectually stimulating. I learn a lot. I see all kinds of statistics. I now consider myself an accomplished economist because of the Federal Reserve. I have my own postulates. Now I have these beautiful, unbiased, and unvarnished bits of information from the Fed to put into a matrix. They do things like, did tariffs change your capital investment? And they have so many different industries to survey. Like, "yes," "no," or "undecided." So, I said, "If you think about a big-picture strategy, in all likelihood some tariffs will have a negative impact on the economy. But the time you want to do that is when we are roaring because tariffs tend to slow down the fast growth. It makes no sense to negotiate strategy when you have a down economy. So, rev up the economy and you can do all kinds of things."

PATRICK: Some believe that as America roars America will have to sustain the rest of the world's economies. Do you have a comment?

MICHAEL: Not to sustain, but it will help. For whatever reason, humans are operated by, "I gotta." "I gotta do this. I gotta do that. I gotta make payroll. I gotta be competitive. I gotta make money. I gotta." And as a company that I'm running, you would like to have these impenetrable barriers where you can coast. I've never found a business that you just coast. Not much happens until "you gotta." If you don't "gotta," you tend not to. So, you "gotta." So, when other countries start to see that they don't have these impenetrable barriers, they don't "gotta." If you think about it, how much of the world is still operating off the subsidies from the USA after WWII? We should wake up and realize these countries are not going to raise their hand and say, "We are all set now, thanks. We don't want those subsidies anymore." Nobody does that! Nobody does that.

PATRICK: Why?

MICHAEL: Because it's there! And it's easy! Now, finally we are disrupting that.

(Michael thinks for a second and drags on his cigarette.)

In the big picture, it may have made sense for NAFTA. And now you've had enough of a head start to compete on your own. That's when you really have free trade. And China? It was a hole in the boat. It was leaking out. And China is buying our T-bills. We are paying them interest! So now, two holes in the boat!

PATRICK: What can we say now about your beloved Cleveland?

MICHAEL: Well, I can start by saying, the very first of the 16 Federal Reserve Committees came out of this region. Just keep in mind this was probably 25 years ago. And maybe this story will help sum up our position. So, because big established companies tend to skew the statistics of what's happening at the grassroots level in a certain way, Sandra Pianalto (President & CEO, Federal Reserve Bank of Cleveland, 2003 to 2014) was tired of seeing our region in the red. Nearly all regions were in the green after the last economic boom except ours. So, she needed to find out why. A special roundtable had been invited from all around Greater Cleveland. Mal Mixon, founder of Invacare, and Michael Feuer co-founder OfficeMax and a few others were to comment on why Cleveland, which was a big portion of Ohio, was lagging. This study took a great deal of time and effort, and Sandra deserves all the credit. Here is what they found. Ohio was a net benefactor of "outsourcing," and that more things were happening from Ohio than were outsourced away. So that's not it. And then they said it was because jobs were leaving. Well, no, the Ohio region actually had a stubbornness for keeping jobs. And the fault in Northeastern Ohio wasn't due to bad PR that you would see on TV or headlines. The end result was our region scored poorly on new job creation. Every other region had more negatives: volatility, outsourcing, insourcing, export, import, leaving the area, that kind of stuff. Cleveland actually scored very, very high in outsourcing, but the one thing we were very, very low on was the creation of new jobs and new technologies and new smaller companies that tend to grow. So, Cardinal and others are helping reverse that negative. Actually, with Visa buying my company, they have embraced Cleveland. They plan on making Cleveland the home of all cyber authentication worldwide.

PATRICK: Maybe we should end it here. But, before we go, Michael, you seem to have this uncanny effect on employees, board members, and even Loretta Mester and Sandra Pianalto.

MICHAEL: You mean like bring out the best in others and making them stretch for higher goals for the good of the business, etc.?

PATRICK: EXACTLY! So, try to imagine how good this book would be if I was writing about someone else? (Patrick winks)

MICHAEL and PATRICK: (LAUGHS, LAUGHS, LAUGHS!)

End of the transcript.

Just moments later, Michael invites me to play golf. Finally, we get to hit the links! My daughter loves that phrase, "hit the links." And, what a treat! A perfect fall day for golf; and guess what? I did not have a hole-in-one. But Michael did have a birdie on Hole 17, a par 3. That's a two! For those who love golf, 17 at Kirtland Country Club is not just your average par 3. It's an adventure into the very fabric of one's soul. Hole 17 at Kirtland is one of the best golf holes in the world.

The tee box is somewhat elevated as we gaze nearly 200 yards to a green that sits like a large basket amongst a surrounding hillside. A forest of trees is along the length of the left side and around the back of the green. However, the right side is completely open, but covered with tall grass. At the tee box the hole slopes down at first, and then from there it gently rolls up over little mounds. It is breathtaking, especially when the tall grasses sway on the invisible breeze that swirls in the canyon. Just in front of the green there is a glimpse of respite for the player, with a large patch of some agreeable short cut grass. This perfectly mown approach rises to the huge but slender putting surface. The green itself is nearly 40 yards long and is shaped like a kidney bean. The middle pinches in on the right side and the whole green slopes dramatically from back to front. Sometimes golfers accidently putt their ball off the green. It's somewhat funny, but not to a golfer. Some see the comedy, watching their opponent's ball roll off the green, but they dare not laugh. The laws of gravity apply to everyone!

The huge majestic trees on the hillside have been standing for well over 200 years. These are the living heirs from the original massive forest for which Cleveland is famous. In the 18th century, robust travelers going west nicknamed the settlement that became known as Cleveland as "the forest city."

Mortals worship here at hole 17 on a regular basis. Ironically, the bells from the renowned Church of Jesus Christ of Latter-Day Saints clang loudly every Sunday. These bells serve as a reminder to "thank God" and not thyself for any score less than bogey!

Kirtland's 17 is basically just a sliver of salvageable landscape modified by man. The short grasses are dwarfed by surrounding forest, tall grasses and sand. Bunkers, sometimes called "sand traps," encircle the green on all sides. Each bunker grows in size as we travel around the green. The first bunker, front left, is very small, not much bigger than a kitchenette you would find in an apartment in New York City. Most golfers don't even notice it. Why? Because the bunker on the right is about the size of a subway station you might find in New York City. And, just like a subway station, players have been known to disappear for extended periods of time. Maybe this story illustrates the authority and respect golfers have of Kirtland's hole 17.

On one occasion, a very fine player hit his ball into the huge bunker on the right. He was a few over par for the day. After several minutes, still no golfer returned from the sand bunker dungeon. Surely he's OK. Nonetheless a caddie was sent into the depths to take a look. Maybe the man needed some help. The caddie reemerged all alone. He said the sand was a mess. The caddie used the word 'war,' to describe the condition of the sand. The caddie then presented a broken Wilson golf club. This was obviously from the player in question. The group was confused, and no one knew what to do. A few moments later, the players, fearing the worst, transformed into a search party. Through the woods and across the hills they went. Twenty minutes later the poor man was found. He was resting at the base of a huge tree. He was covered in sand! He was clammy, disheveled and mumbling incoherently. The group quickly rushed the golfer to the men's locker house. They called a doctor and got him a stiff drink.

THE END

Credits

This book would not have been possible without the dedication and foresight of the whole Keresman family. I would especially like to thank Michael's wife, Liz, and daughters, Katelyn, Jaclyn and Joslyn. Perhaps Michael said it best in his Lake Erie College commencement address (which appears in chapter 7 of this book): "Right now, I'm president of something called Three by Three Ventures. And Three by Three Ventures means my wife, Liz, and I raised three wonderful children—three 'A-plus' girls. Also, we were part of three successful business ventures. As I stand here, and the older I get, when I look at the value of all those things, I think the first three (our daughters) were the more important."

Interviews, Alphabetical

Christopher Baird
Chandra Balasubramanian
Mary Ballard
Gary Bender
Howard Bobrow
James Boland
Jeff Bowman
Ed Brandon
Lee Burdman
Jon Dick
Erik Enright
Dan Filippi
Renee Galinac
Eric Goodman
Jaime Goodman
Gary Gordan
Katie Hale

Jamie Henry
Ron Hess Jr.
John Jelenic
Janet Kapostay
Jaclyn Keresman
Josie Keresman
Katie Keresman
Lizzie Keresman
Matthew Keresman
Maureen Keresman
Michael Keresman
Tara Lavelle
Crystal Leidy
Colt McCutcheon
Marc Morgenstern
Steve Mott
Jeff Neville

Eric Nuemore
William O'Riordan
Larry Pollock
Bruce Poore
Adam Ratica
Kent Richardson
Phil Romano
Bill Sanford

Nikko Scaife
John Schick
Tim Sherwin
Mary Smoley
Paul Turgeon
Larry Weber
Tim Wolfe
Mike Yakel

Other Sources

Two publications were helpful sources of information about Lake Erie College / Lake Erie Female Seminary:

The Role of Female Seminaries on the Road to Social Justice for Women by Kristen Welch (Author), Abraham Ruelas (Author), Susie C. Stanley, (Foreword).

"The Dangerous Experiment: The Building of the Seven Sister Colleges Dr. Helen Horowitz" by Dr. Helen Horowitz, published online at: www.womenshistory.org/articles/dangerous-experiment

Additional Acknowledgments

Jaime Goodman
Jim Boland
David Gray
Frank Lewis

Adam Ratica
Michael Roach
Patrick Roach

Special Thanks

Mike & Liz Keresman
Lisa Alexander
Mackenzie Alexander
Brynn Alexander
Lou & Reece Alexander
Joe Znidarsic
John Mino
Bill Coughlin
Mike & Sus Costigan

Steve Eggelston
Peter Wray

Legenderry Communications Staff

Natalie Yuhas, *Chief Research / Editor*

Renee Gerhart, *Assistant Editor*

Frannie Foltz, *Assistant Editor*

Leslie Langnau, *Assistant Editor*

Susan Mitchell, *Assistant Editor*

Diana Frankhauser, *Assistant*

Daniel McMullen, *Legal Consultant*

Steve Galbincea, *Research Assistant*

Tania Saliba, *Artwork*

Red Bicycle Media

The Staff @ Money 20/20

Made in the USA
Monee, IL
07 June 2021